COOKING WITH THE
Two Fat Ladies

Cooking with the Two Fat Ladies

JENNIFER PATERSON &
CLARISSA DICKSON WRIGHT

press
élan
A GENERAL PUBLISHING IMPRINT

NOTE: All recipes serve four unless otherwise stated.

First published in Canada in 1998 by
élan press, an imprint of General Publishing Co. Limited
30 Lesmill Road, Toronto, Canada M3B 2T6

10 9 8 7 6 5 4 3

First published in the United Kingdom in 1996 by Ebury Press
Random House, 20 Vauxhall Bridge Road, London SW1V 2SA

Random House UK Limited Reg. No. 954009

Canadian Cataloguing in Publication Data is available from the
National Library of Canada

ISBN 1-55144-1845

Food photography by James Murphy
Food styling by Janet Smith
Styling by Roisin Nield
Cover design by Slatter-Anderson
Text designed by Paul Wood

Printed and bound in Portugal by Printer Portuguesa L.d.a.

Contents

*H*OW IT ALL BEGAN...

Finding the right contributors for a program is a skill all television researchers worth their salt must acquire early in their careers. One of my formative professional experiences was working on a food series where my brief was to unearth non-professional cooks from a wide variety of backgrounds, with passions for particular vegetables, who would be prepared to share their recipes with the TV audience. After the first half-dozen people had been filmed, our producer took me aside and pointed out gently that I really needed to rethink my approach to finding interviewees for the programs. Why, she wanted to know, were all my chosen favorites for the series "large, posh, middle-aged women?"

One of the consequences of this professional *faux pas* was meeting Clarissa Dickson Wright, or Clarissa Cardoon as she became known in our office. Her enthusiasm for that majestic vegetable came oozing through the TV screen, and the production team became avid devotees of the huge edible thistles for at least a month.

Clarissa and I kept in touch after the series was over and, as I moved from food program to food program, I would often phone her for a gastronomic titbit or for verification of some obscure historical culinary detail to include in a program or script. Clarissa always seemed to know the answer – or on the rare occasions she did not, she always knew which book or publication would provide one.

We had talked about working together again, but finding the right idea was elusive. The credit for discovering Clarissa's ideal television partner must go to my dear friend Basil Comely (who also seems rather inclined toward large, posh, middle-aged women). He was introduced to Jennifer Paterson at a party and urged me to meet her. We had lunch. "Are you married?" Jennifer asked me over my oxtail. "No," I replied. "Well my advice to someone of your age (31 at the time) is to find yourself a nice poof." She's introduced me to many since, but, oddly, none of them have proposed.

Jennifer and Clarissa record the
program's title song, with the
help of Pete Baikie, who wrote it

Basil and I spent a few wine-sodden evenings plotting and planning the beginnings of "Two Fat Ladies," but it was not long before our palates parted us professionally. As canned soup and potato chips are his favorite foods, Basil is the first to admit that food programs are not really where his heart lies.

Clarissa, Jennifer, and I made a pilot program for the BBC. It was a colorful shoot. Although Jennifer is an accomplished motorbike rider, at the time her experience of traveling with a sidecar attached was limited. After a number of perfect "takes," we had one final shot to achieve. Jennifer was to drive herself and Clarissa toward the camera, stop, and then deliver a few lines. As the cameraman and I stood behind the camera watching our ladies speeding toward us, our sound operator, who could hear things that we could not, began waving his arms frantically. Jennifer had gotten the brake and gears mixed up (quite understandably, of course, as they were the other way around on her own bike).

We all lived to tell the tale to anyone who would listen. The motorbike and sidecar mowed down the camera tripod and disappeared into the distance. It is debatable whether we would still have had two presenters for the series had it not been for an obliging flagpole. Copious bunches of flowers were showered on our location co-ordinator's father, who spent many a weekend repairing his 40-year-old, classic AJS motorbike and sidecar without a grumble.

The pilot program was sent to the BBC and given a few private screenings to sympathetic friends and colleagues. There was little doubt that our two fat ladies were enormously entertaining, but would their completely uncompromising approach to food and cooking be acceptable to those in control of the purse strings? How would they react to Jennifer and Clarissa's militant anti-vegetarianism? What would be made of their constant ridicule of all the recent press reports of what constitutes a healthy diet? My own doubts about the possibilities of making the series increased when I showed the pilot to a respected colleague whose response was, "Oh Pat, what have you done?"

After a month of knuckle-munching anxiety, the BBC gave us the green light. Making the program has been the most enjoyable production experience I have known. A shoot is not usually an environment characterized by hilarity and good humor, but I have seldom laughed as much during filming as on this series. This poor director has had terrible tricks played on her by mischievous presenters. I have been made a laughing stock in front of the crew. I have been mercilessly teased about my scripts, albeit with warmth and affection. But the greatest reward of working with Jennifer and Clarissa has been their total lack of "presenteritis," a word sometimes used in the television business to describe presenters with an inflated sense of their own importance. The team spirit of our "two fat ladies," their unfailing good humor, and lack of airs and graces are rare qualities to find in screen "stars" (and it had better stay like that, ladies, or else)!

Patricia Llewellyn
Producer

FISH AND SHELLFISH

CLARISSA WRITES: Surrounded as we are by water, we are terribly served for fish. My sister once lived in the center of Spain, and the fish merchants came up from the coast three times a week with live fish. Here, the average fishmonger in large towns, when you can find one, offers a limited choice, and the fish is not always in its first flush of freshness. Supermarket fish is usually a disgrace and a victim of some central buying and distribution policy, which means it has traveled the country more times than Jennifer and I have in this series! The most useful tool in judging the freshness of fish is the nose, quickly followed by the eyes. The chances of your being allowed to smell an individual fish in a supermarket are slight, but you can challenge your fishmonger who will usually permit you. Of course, if you make a friend of him you won't need to check.

Buying monkfish on the quay at Mevagissey, in Cornwall

As I write this introduction, I am sitting in the Sharksfin Hotel in Mevagissey, having just enjoyed a well-earned hot bath laced with Epsom salts. We have spent the afternoon at sea with two splendid crab fishermen. Jennifer and I were both soaked to the skin and had a high old time singing (at least Jennifer did) sea chanties with our new friends. The pots held a good haul of crabs and three of what passes for good-sized lobsters these days. When

Queen Victoria visited Edinburgh they served a hundred-pound lobster as the centerpiece of her civic banquet!

The port is quiet today because many fishermen have gone up to London to petition Parliament to support our fishing industry. Yesterday I spoke to a visitor who had grown up in Cornwall – he was only in his sixties – and he said, "It is impossible to believe that they have almost fished the seas dry." The best way to protect our fishing industry is, of course, to buy fresh fish. Then demand will keep our supplies from being exported.

Neither of us much believe the pronouncements of *soi-disant* health experts – we both eat fish because we love it, the fresher the better. So for once we are not out of step with these "experts" in believing in the health benefits of fish. However, do not bypass advice to eat oily fish by taking fish oil tablets – it isn't the same.

We have seen some wonderful fish since we have been here, such as the underrated coley, which Jennifer turned into a luscious fish pie. Coley – similar to pollack – is still amazingly underpriced and very good. We've also seen the hideous monkfish, the true denizen of the deep with its huge head and delicious flesh, ling cod, John Dory – still bearing St. Peter's thumbprint – the sad-faced little gurnards, which Jennifer loves so much, and so many more.

Jennifer purchases a coley the size of "a bloody great mermaid"

In the "Mr. Bistro" restaurant on the quay, where we ate many meals, Sally, the owner, cooked us wonderful fish so fresh it needed little more than seasoning, and we laughed and flirted with Lawrence and Trevor and John *et al.* You don't need to go abroad to meet handsome fishermen.

In our recipes we have tried to give you a variety of uses for different fish, to suit all pockets and occasions. There are really only two things to remember with fish: buy it as fresh as possible (we have given you tips to help with this) and please don't overcook it – it is better to err on the side of caution and undercook it, because a very hot serving dish can easily remedy that situation.

Off to buy monkfish

*W*hen I cooked on a charter yacht in the United States, I wanted to bring back some steamer clams and Maine lobster for my brother, to convince him that New England seafood was the best. The customs officer heard the lobsters scrabbling away in my bag and said I couldn't bring them through if they were alive. Can I if they are dead, I asked? Yes, said the customs officer. So I took off my brooch in order to drive the pin through the brain of each lobster. What are you doing? said the officer. I was planning to kill them, I replied. Not in front of me, you're not, says the officer. So I got them through alive.

Clarissa

(*left*)
Descending the harbor wall at Mevagissey to go crabbing

(*bottom left*)
On the boat with fishermen and camera crew

(*below*)
Lovely weather for it: Jennifer and Clarissa cook mussels in the pouring rain on Hemmick Beach

Jennifer's Fishing Experiences

I used to collect shrimp when I was little, at Fairlight, near Hastings, and when I was a little girl in Shanghai Gwon, I used to go walking with my Amah to pick up jellyfish for jellyfish soup. I also used to go out at night with the fishermen in Taormina to catch tuna, which they did by grabbing them by the eyes.

*S*ALMON TRAFALGAR

I suspect this dish is older than 1812, and was renamed in the wave of patriotism
that surrounded Nelson's victory. The elderberries make an unusual sauce, which I like very much.
It also satisfies my need to do something with my elderberries.

FOR THE ELDERBERRY SAUCE:

**3 pounds elderberries (to make
about 2½ cups of juice)**

6 whole cloves

**1-ounce piece of fresh
ginger root**

1¾ cups sugar

a 3-pound salmon or sea trout

½ cup (1 stick) butter, melted

juice of 1 lemon

salt and freshly ground pepper

FOR THE WHITE FISH SAUCE:

2 tablespoons butter

3 tablespoons flour

white wine or fish stock

1 tablespoon minced parsley

2½ tablespoons capers, chopped

First make the elderberry sauce: place the fruit in a bowl and
bruise with a wooden spoon. Add 2 teaspoons water, then cook in
a double boiler, or in a bowl set over a pan of boiling water, until
the juices flow freely. Pulp again by mashing with a spoon. Strain
through a sieve lined with cheesecloth and return to the pan. You
should have about 2½ cups of juice.

Wrap the cloves and ginger in a cheesecloth bag, add to the
strained juice, and simmer for 15 minutes. Add the sugar and stir
until it has dissolved. Discard the cheesecloth bag. Pour the sauce
into sterilized jars. Cover and refrigerate, or process in boiling
water to cover for 20 minutes to preserve indefinitely.

Have your fishmonger clean your salmon, skin it, and fillet it into
two fillets. (Before you accuse me of elitism, I do this myself.)
Place the fillets in a buttered baking dish, add the melted butter
and lemon juice, and season with salt and pepper. Cover and bake
in a preheated oven at 350°F for 15–20 minutes.

Make a roux with the butter and flour and add the cooking juices
from the fish (add some white wine or fish stock to make 1¼
cups). Add the parsley and capers and heat through. Add
elderberry sauce to taste. If you prefer a thinner, simple sauce, just
add the parsley and capers to the cooking juices, reduce, and
flavor with some of the elderberry sauce. Serve the fish with the
sauce poured over it.

CDW

CRAB PÂTÉ

A really good fresh crab, with its magnificent claws, always brings joy to my heart. In fact, I think they are even more delectable than lobsters, which can often be rather tough, though a perfect one is sublime – straight from the pot to the table. The following recipe will make crab go a lot further than just tucking in with mayonnaise, besides being very delicious with a fine, strong, gutsy flavor.

1 pound crab meat
(if there is any brown meat,
be sure to include it, too)

¾ cup (1½ sticks) unsalted butter

4 extra large egg yolks

¼ cup heavy cream

3 tablespoons medium sherry

¼ cup freshly grated
Parmesan cheese

hot pepper sauce

lemon juice

Melt the butter in a saucepan big enough to receive the rest of the ingredients. Stir in the crab meat (you can even use frozen in a pinch). Heat gently, stirring all together. Beat the egg yolks, cream, and sherry together, then pour into the crab mixture. Continue to cook and stir until it all thickens. Keep the heat low – we don't want any crumbling. Add the cheese and stir until melted. Take off the heat and season with pepper sauce and lemon juice to taste. Allow to cool.

Give the mixture a final good stirring, then pour into a soufflé dish and chill for 6 hours or overnight. Eat with hot brown toast and butter, though it hardly needs it.

JP

*B*ACALHAU (SALT COD) À MODA DE PINHAL NORTE

I lived in Porto, Portugal, for two years a long time ago and have always loved it – the people, the towns, the country, and the food, which is streets ahead of any Spanish cooking. *Bacalhau* is the national dish and there are 365 ways of cooking it, so they say. It has a strong, pungent flavor and I love it. This is a particularly interesting method of cooking it. The turnips give a marvelous taste to the mixture.

2 pounds salt cod

2 pounds young turnips

2 pounds potatoes

salt and freshly ground pepper

2 large onions, thinly sliced

olive oil

butter

4 hard-cooked eggs

black olives

You can buy salt cod in Caribbean, Italian, and Asian markets. Rigid as cement, it looks gray and ghastly and smells worse, but do not flinch. Have it cut into a useful size for soaking. Soak in cold water, with frequent changes, for 24–36 hours. If you have a running stream, so much the better. Boil the rinsed fish for 20–30 minutes until flakeable. Remove skin and bones and flake the flesh.

Peel the turnips and boil until tender, then cut into thick slices. Boil the potatoes in their skins, drain, peel, and mash fairly roughly. Season. Fry the onions gently in olive oil for 10 minutes.

Generously butter an earthenware baking dish large enough to hold all the ingredients. Spread half the mashed potatoes on the bottom of the dish and grind black pepper all over them. Lay the flaked fish on the potatoes, then the turnips. Chop the eggs and crumble them over the turnips, then spread with the onions and, finally, with the rest of the potatoes. Pour about ⅔ cup of good fruity olive oil all over the surface and dot with butter.

Heat thoroughly in a preheated oven at 350°F for thirty minutes. This is a great big wonderful rustic dish. Serve it scattered with black olives and with some good fresh spinach on the side.

JP

$\mathcal{S}$ALTFISH CAKES WITH RED PEPPER TAPENADE

We have lost the habit of eating salted fish, although stockfish was one of the great staples of our diet in the days before refrigeration. I thought this up on a recent trip to Barbados, where saltfish remains one of the mainstays of the island food supply, as it has been since the slave days of the eighteenth century. Saltfish must be well soaked – 24 hours in cold water changed at regular intervals is about right. The idea of using red peppers in tapenade I learned from that hero of late-twentieth-century cooking, the brilliant Robert Carrier.

FOR THE RED PEPPER TAPENADE:

2 red bell peppers

1½ cups black olives, pitted

1 tablespoon Bordeaux mustard

2-ounce can anchovy fillets, drained

⅓ cup capers

⅔ cup olive oil

1 pound salt cod, soaked (see p.17)

1 pound pale yellow-fleshed sweet potatoes (or ordinary potatoes if not available)

6–8 scallions, minced

2 eggs

salt and freshly ground pepper

oil

First make the tapenade. Roast the peppers in the broiler until charred; when cool, slip off the skins, then chop them. Place all the ingredients, except the olive oil, in a mortar or food processor and pound or process together. Drizzle in the oil slowly as for mayonnaise and blend until the tapenade has a grainy, fairly coarse texture. Keep in a cool place.

Simmer your soaked cod in fresh water for 10 minutes, then drain, remove skin and bones, and flake with a fork.

Ensure your sweet potatoes are fresh or they will discolor. Peel and boil in salted water until soft – they take about twice as long as "Irish Potatoes" (this is what white potatoes are called in Barbados). Drain and mash well.

At this stage I usually put it all in a food processor. Mix together the fish, mashed sweet potatoes, scallions, and eggs, and season to taste. Form into small fishcakes and fry in hot oil until golden brown on both sides. Serve hot with the tapenade.

$\mathcal{P}$ASTAI GOCOS

Our director, the stylish, energetic, enthusiastic Pat Llewellyn, is Welsh, so I am making a special effort to remember some of my Welsh dishes to show we love her really, even if we are mean to her when she has us standing on one leg for half an hour. This is a traditional Welsh cockle pie which can be served hot or cold. The Welsh have their own onion, also known as an Oriental or Japanese bunching onion, which is perfect for this dish but not readily available, so use scallions or chives.

**2½ pounds cockles
or small hardshell clams**

pastry for a two-crust pie

**1 cup fresh chives or chopped
scallions**

½ pound Canadian bacon, diced

salt and freshly ground pepper

1 egg

Cook the cockles in 1¼ cups water for 15 minutes. Drain, keeping the cooking liquid. Remove the cockles from their shells.

Roll out half of the pastry and use to line the bottom of a 5-cup capacity deep-dish pie pan or baking dish. Put in a layer of cockles and then a layer of chives or scallions followed by a layer of bacon. Continue to build up layers. Finally, pour over the strained cooking liquid and season well.

Roll out the rest of the pastry and cut into strips to make a lattice on the top of the pie. Brush with lightly beaten egg and bake in a preheated oven at 400°F for 30–40 minutes.

CDW

*F*ISH PIE

Like most people, I always welcome fish pie as one of the most comforting of foods. This is rather a grandiose one and is splendid to eat on Good Friday after a day of fasting, or on Christmas Eve before midnight mass, or, for that matter, any time you fancy it.

1 pound pollack fillets

1 pound smoked haddock fillet (finan haddie)

2–3 pounds fresh leaf spinach

½ cup (1 stick) butter, plus extra for the top

salt and freshly ground pepper

grated nutmeg

1 large mild onion, thinly sliced

3 tablespoons flour

3¾ cups milk

1 bayleaf

1–2 teaspoons anchovy paste

1 big bunch of parsley, minced

6 sea scallops

½ pound peeled cooked shrimp

1 cup freshly grated Parmesan cheese

Put the pollack and smoked haddock into a large pan and pour boiling water over just to cover. Simmer very gently for 10 minutes. Turn it all out into a clean sink and leave until the fish is cool enough to handle, then remove skin and any bones. Flake the fish onto a plate and reserve.

Wash the spinach thoroughly and place in a saucepan – do not add any water. Cook gently until it collapses, then raise the heat and cook until done, about 3 minutes. Drain well, pressing the liquid out. Return the spinach to the saucepan with 4 tablespoons butter and season to taste with salt, pepper, and nutmeg. Spread the spinach evenly on the bottom of a well-buttered baking dish large enough to hold the rest of the ingredients.

Melt the remaining 4 tablespoons of butter in a saucepan and cook the onion gently until translucent. Add the flour and stir to make a roux. Have the milk heated to a simmer and add it little by little until you have a smooth white sauce. Pop in the bayleaf and let it simmer for half an hour, stirring now and then.

Stir the anchovy paste and parsley into the sauce, and season with salt and pepper. Mix in the flaked fish and pour onto the spinach. Slice the scallops in half horizontally and distribute over the fish. Scatter the shrimp over the top, sprinkle with the Parmesan, and dot with a little extra butter. Bake in a preheated oven at 400°F for 20–30 minutes until heated through and browned on the top. Serve with a purée of potato and a tomato salad.

JP

Mackerel Run Down

In Barbados a "run down" or an "oil down" is the name for a stew combining different ingredients. Pat Byres, the famous West Indian silversmith, gave me this recipe. It sounds strange to our palates, but it is very good, and as mackerel are only edible plain if they are straight from the sea, it is an excellent way of dealing with the ones we can buy.

2 onions, minced

6 tomatoes, seeded and minced

oil

4 medium mackerel, filleted

1 can coconut milk

a dash of West Indian hot pepper sauce

salt and freshly ground pepper

In a frying pan fry up the onions and tomatoes in a little oil. When the onions are soft, add the mackerel and sauté slightly. Add the coconut milk and hot sauce. The amount of hot sauce is really to your individual taste, but be cautious. Season. Cover and cook gently for 15 minutes.

CDW

Clarissa's tip

With fish, freshness is paramount. Use your nose and eyes. The fish's eyes should be glistening, the gills should be pink, and it should never smell "fishy," but should smell of the sea.

MARINATED MACKEREL (POOR MAN'S GRAVADLAX)

When mackerel are fine, fat, and plentiful, there is no better fish to be bought for the price. They are not only beautiful to look at, but are one of the oily fish meant to be so good for you. They must be spanking fresh. I remember once in Ullapool, in Scotland, with its fishing harbor and boats all lined up, that it was impossible to buy a fish in the shops, such is the waywardness of bureaucracy, but you could sometimes gather them when they were dropped by a passing seagull. Slightly damaged maybe, but the fish couldn't be fresher – they were delicious beyond compare. Marinated like this they are every bit as good as their grander cousins.

**2 large mackerel
(about 1 pound each)**

2 tablespoons sugar

3 tablespoons coarse sea salt

**2 teaspoons minced dill
(fresh or freeze-dried)**

Have the fish halved and filleted, but leave the skins on. Mix all the other ingredients together and rub into both sides of the fillets, leaving the surplus on the cut sides. Stick the sides together to form a whole fish, place in a shallow dish, cover with foil, and place another dish of similar size and shape on top filled with weights of some sort (jars or cans of food). Leave in a cool place for 24 hours.

Unwrap; drain off all the liquid and scrape off any of the mixture. Wrap the fish in plastic wrap and chill well or even half freeze (this makes the slicing easier). When the fish is very firm with cold, turn the cut sides upward and slice down to the skin somewhat diagonally to produce paper thin, almost translucent slices, excluding the skin as for smoked salmon.

Serve with brown bread and butter and the following sauce: Beat 1 egg with 2 tablespoons Dijon mustard, and add ½ teaspoon superfine sugar and 1 tablespoon of white wine vinegar. Now slowly beat in about 6 tablespoons of olive oil as if you were making mayonnaise. Season with a touch of salt and lemon juice and stir in some minced fresh dill.

DEVILED SMOKED SALMON

I am so addicted to smoked salmon that I find it hard to serve any other appetizer at my dinner table. Choosing smoked salmon is both a joy and a quandary, especially since I moved to Scotland, where there are a variety of smokings. My beloved fishmonger, Mr. Clarke of Fisher Row, Musselburgh, smokes wild fish to his own cure. My friend, Johnnie Noble from Loch Fyne, now produces Bradan Orach, which has a longer, more traditional smoke than his ordinary London smoke, which was introduced by the Russian Jews who came over in the 1890s. London Smoke is oilier and more delicate than the traditional Scottish smoke. It is, in fact, what we think of as smoked salmon. Most of the Scottish smokeries have their own, individual product. As long as you avoid non-Scots smoked salmon, and most supermarkets' own brand, it is a great adventure. I usually serve more than one type and end up with leftovers which I treat thus:

4 tablespoons softened butter

8 slices of wholegrain toast, crusts removed

salt and freshly ground pepper

1 pound smoked salmon

½ cup curry butter (1 stick softened butter mixed with curry powder and cayenne pepper to taste)

Butter the toast on one side, and sprinkle with salt and pepper. Cover with thin slices of smoked salmon and spread with curry butter. Place in a preheated oven at 400°F to heat for about 5 minutes.

CDW

---

*M*y father had a Scottish friend who would prepare salmon for his dinner parties. He would catch the salmon himself, but when he served it he would surround the fish with black crepe and laurel wreaths, and explain that they were mourning the death of the fish. The salmon was usually delicious, but eating it in a state of mourning put my father off his dinner.

Clarissa

*M*ARINATED LOCH FYNE KIPPERS

Whichever kippers you use, make sure they are the true smoked ones. These are almost silvery in hue, unlike the dark brown variety, which are dyed.

kippers

olive oil

lemon juice

sugar

freshly ground black pepper

Cut the tails off the fish and skin them from the tail end (this is very easy). Remove the fillets from the bones and lay them in a shallow dish.

In a jar, make a mixture of olive oil and lemon juice, using 1 spoonful of juice to every 6 spoonsful of oil, and season with a pinch of sugar and a good grinding of black pepper. Mix together, then pour over the fish. Leave to marinate for at least 2 hours.

Serve chilled, with a good potato salad dressed with the same vinaigrette, flavored with Dijon mustard to taste. Sprinkle with minced dill.

JP

$\mathcal{S}$CALLOPS WITH LEEKS

I have used vermouth in this dish, which gives a good flavor. I love having vermouth around for cooking, as I am not tempted to drink it.

12 fresh sea scallops on their shells

8 young leeks

4 tablespoons unsalted butter

salt and freshly ground pepper

2 shallots, minced

⅔ cup dry white wine

¼ cup dry vermouth

⅔ cup heavy cream

1 bunch of parsley, flat-leaf preferably, roughly minced

Remove the scallops from their shells or ask your fishmonger to do this. Separate the white flesh from the roe (if still there), and detach the hard skin around the whites and the tiny black sac from the roe. Wash clean under a running tap. Halve the whites horizontally. Leave to dry off on some paper towel.

Wash the leeks and discard the green parts (you can use them for soup or stock). Slice the white stems lengthwise into narrow strips about 2 inches long. Place in a saucepan with 2 tablespoons of the butter, a pinch of salt, and ½ cup of water. Cover and simmer for 20 minutes. Keep hot.

In another pan, melt the rest of the butter and then gently cook the shallots until they are soft. Add the wine, vermouth, and the scallops, with their roe if available. Bring just to boiling point, then turn the heat very low and simmer for exactly 2 minutes, or less if the scallops are small.

Remove the leeks from their liquid using a slotted spoon and place in a heated dish. With the same implement place the scallops on top. Add the leek juice to the scallop juice and boil briskly until the liquid is reduced to ½ cup. Pour in the cream, bring back to a boil, and bubble for a moment or two. Season with salt and pepper. Pour over the arranged scallops and leeks. Scatter the minced parsley over all.

JP

LADY LLANOVER'S SALMON

Our beloved Pat Llewellyn is convinced that only the Welsh cook salmon in red wine. She may be right. Certainly the renowned Lady Llanover did. It adds a richness to the fish that is quite unique.

6 tablespoons butter

2 tablespoons flour

1 onion, minced

1 pound mushrooms, sliced

1 garlic clove, minced

sprig of fresh rosemary

a 2-pound, middle-cut piece of salmon, skinned

½ bottle of red wine

Work 2 tablespoons of the butter with the flour into a paste (*beurre manié*) and set aside. Fry the onion and mushrooms in the remaining butter. When soft, add the garlic and rosemary. Pour the fried onion mixture into a casserole, add the skinned salmon, pour the red wine over, and leave to marinate for 2 hours.

Put the casserole on the heat, bring the liquid to a boil, and simmer gently for 15 minutes. Lift out the salmon and fillet it, but leave it in one piece. Keep warm. Strain the sauce and return it to the casserole. Reduce the sauce, gradually whisking in the *beurre manié* until it is the consistency of thin cream.

Put the strained vegetables from the casserole in a serving dish, place the salmon on top, and pour over the sauce. Serve hot.

CDW

Clarissa's tip

To tell wild salmon from farmed, pick the fish up by its tail.
If it slips through your fingers, it's farmed: farmed salmon has
no tail muscle.

LOU'S NORWEGIAN FISH PUDDING

This receipt was handed down to Roald Dahl by his mother and grandmother.
He was a very good cook himself and thoroughly enjoyed preparing great feasts for his friends and family.

½ pound smoked, undyed
haddock fillet

½ pound smoked cod or white
fish fillet

1¼ cups milk

¾ cup heavy cream

1½ tablespoons potato flour

2 teaspoons salt

freshly ground black pepper

minced parsley

FOR THE SAUCE:

2 tablespoons butter

2 tablespoons flour

1½ cups milk, warmed

1 tablespoon tomato paste

2 tablespoons dry sherry

juice of ½ lemon

3 ounces smoked oysters or mussels

½ pound peeled cooked shrimp,
plus more for garnish

You can make this pudding in a 1½-quart ring mold or 6 individual molds. Skin the two fishes. Cut, place in a food processor, and process for a few seconds, or mince finely. Add the milk, cream, potato flour, salt, and a good grinding of pepper. Process again. Put the mixture into the lightly oiled mold (or molds). Cover with foil and place in a roasting pan half filled with water. Bake in a preheated oven at 400°F for about 20 minutes until firm to the touch.

Meanwhile, prepare the sauce. Make a roux in a saucepan with the butter and flour, then add the warmed milk little by little to form a smooth sauce. Add the tomato paste, sherry, and lemon juice. Bring to a simmer and cook for 20 minutes. Check for seasoning. Add the smoked oysters or mussels and the shrimp. Let them heat through, but on no account boil.

Go around the pudding with a knife and unmold onto a warmed platter. Pour the sauce over it and sprinkle with minced parsley and a few extra shrimp. Serve immediately with a watercress salad.

JP

POTTED SHRIMP

I am extremely fond of a good potted shrimp, which is becoming more and more difficult to find. As often as not, it turns out to be a potted prawn or larger shrimp, which is not the same thing at all. They must be the tiny little creatures, so if you ever find them south of Morecambe, seize and pot them. They will keep well and can, of course, be frozen.

1 pound tiny shrimp (peeled weight)

1 cup (2 sticks) butter

1 bayleaf

¼ teaspoon freshly grated nutmeg or mace

freshly ground black pepper

sea salt

cayenne

If the shrimp are frozen, thaw slowly and completely, draining and drying off with paper towels. To clarify the butter, put it in a small saucepan and heat slowly to boiling point. Let it bubble for a few seconds, then strain through a small sieve lined with cheesecloth into a bowl. Leave it to cool and then chill until set.

Tip the butter out of the bowl and scrape off any sediment clinging to the bottom. Put the butter in a bowl set over simmering water. Add the bayleaf, nutmeg or mace, and black pepper and salt to taste. When melted, add the shrimp and gently mix everything together. Leave over the heat for 10 minutes, stirring occasionally. Discard the bayleaf, and spoon the shrimp into a straight-sided dish or individual ramekins. They should be just covered by the butter. Leave to cool, then chill in the refrigerator.

Serve, sprinkled with cayenne, as a first course with warm brown toast, butter, and lemon wedges. The shrimp will keep 2–3 days in the refrigerator, or 2 weeks if totally sealed with more clarified butter.

JP

Jennifer's tip

Crustaceans taste better if they are eaten at room temperature. Too hot they taste of nothing, too cold dulls the flavor. Try storing shellfish in the salad compartment of your refrigerator, but do buy them on the day of eating

$\mathcal{R}$OASTED CONGER EEL

Conger eel is another neglected fish, although when I wrote about it in the *London Evening Standard* I received an enthusiastic crop of letters from England's West Country. This traditional method of cooking eel I found in Dorothy Hartley's *Food in England*. The alcoholic cider helps to cut the gelatinous tendency of the fish. The dish may splatter when cooking, but this can't be helped.

a 12- to 18-inch middle-cut piece of conger eel

1 onion, halved

FOR THE STUFFING:

1 onion, minced

butter

3 cups bread crumbs

2 garlic cloves, minced

double handful of parsley, minced

single handful of fresh sage, minced

salt and freshly ground pepper

1 apple

lard or drippings

1¼ cups hard apple cider

Rub the inside of the fish with the cut sides of the onion, then discard the onion. Make the stuffing by softening the minced onion in butter, then adding the remaining ingredients and frying lightly until golden. Stuff the fish with the stuffing and season. Tie up with string. Cut the apple in half and use it to plug either end of the fish, securing with wooden toothpicks or kebab skewers.

Melt a little lard or drippings in a roasting pan, add the fish, and pour the cider over. Roast in a preheated oven at 350°F for 40 minutes, basting frequently. Serve with a watercress salad or a crisp green vegetable.

CDW

CRAB, CORN, AND CILANTRO FRITTERS

This Indonesian dish is so good that you need to allow about a third for the "Knaves of Hearts" that pass the kitchen as they are being made. The quantities here will make about 45 2-inch fritters.

6 ears of fresh corn

½ cup crab meat

1 medium onion, grated

2 tablespoon minced fresh cilantro

1 teaspoon ground cilantro

2 garlic cloves, minced

3 eggs, lightly beaten

¼ cup flour

salt and freshly ground pepper

peanut oil

Cut the corn kernels from the cob with a sharp knife. Mix with the remaining ingredients, except the oil. Cover and refrigerate for at least half a day.

Heat a tablespoon of oil in a frying pan and drop in tablespoons of the crab and corn batter. Fry briskly till brown, then turn and cook the other side. A splatter lid is useful as the kernels may burst while cooking. Drain the fritters on paper towels and keep warm until all are cooked. Serve as soon as possible.

CDW

The first thing I cooked was a crab. I was nine years old and it was on the beach. I was forced to seek out something to eat as I was staying with my cousin at the time, who was the most appalling cook and always managed to burn everything she prepared. I caught crabs with coathangers from under the rocks, then built a brushwood fire and boiled them in sea-water in a tin.

Clarissa

*G*IGOT OF MONKFISH ROMARIN WITH ANCHOVIES

I love monkfish tail and I love it with anchovies. The edge with rosemary comes from Pat Llewellyn in her cook's hat. The Scots, who have adopted the word *gigot* with gusto and even talk of "gigit chops" for leg cuts of meat, have long attached this term to monkfish. The *haute cuisine* chefs were further behind.

a 2¼-pound monkfish tail

2 ounce can anchovy fillets

6 tablespoons olive oil

juice of 1 lemon

salt and freshly ground pepper

a large bunch of fresh rosemary

FOR THE TOMATO VINAIGRETTE:

⅔ cup olive oil

4 teaspoons wine vinegar

2 tablespoons minced tomatoes

Using a larding needle or a sharp knife, make slits in the fish and insert pieces of anchovy. Marinate the fish in the oil and lemon juice, seasoned with salt and pepper, for at least 2 hours.

Lay the fish on a large bed of rosemary in a roasting pan. Pour more oil over the fish. (It is the presence of fat that releases the essential oils of the rosemary.) Roast in a preheated oven at 350°F for 45 minutes.

To make the tomato vinaigrette, heat the ingredients in a small pan and season to taste.

Transfer the fish to a serving dish and pour the warm vinaigrette over.

CDW

Illustrated on previous pages

*E*GGS DRUMKILBO

A friend asked me to find this receipt, so I asked in vain all the cooks I knew. Then a certain Tom Price, who had read my pleas, sent me the answer. He had had it at some convention at Sandringham hosted by the Prince of Wales for the edification of journalists. Later I received a letter from Lady Elphinstone who actually lives in Drumkilbo. She told me that her uncle's cook was the first perpetrator of this dish, and it was served at Buckingham Palace as part of the wedding breakfast for Princess Anne and Captain Mark Phillips. Isn't that a fine detective story? Here goes…

a 1½–2 pound lobster

½ pound raw shrimp

8 good tomatoes

8 hard-cooked eggs

fresh mayonnaise

a little tomato paste

anchovy paste

Worcestershire sauce

hot pepper sauce

salt and freshly ground pepper

2 tablespoons unflavored gelatin

white wine or water

Cook the lobster and shrimp in boiling water, 10–12 minutes for the lobster, 2–3 minutes for the shrimp. Drain and when cool enough to handle, discard the shells. Dice the flesh of both. Dip the tomatoes into boiling water for half a minute, then skin and seed them. Dice the flesh and add to the lobster and shrimp. Remove the whites from 2 of the eggs and discard. Dice all the yolks and the rest of the whites, and add to the mixture. Mix all the ingredients with sufficient mayonnaise, flavored with tomato paste, anchovy paste, Worcestershire sauce, and hot pepper sauce to taste, to produce a good, fairly stiffish consistency. Check for seasoning.

Dissolve the gelatin in a little boiling white wine or water, but do not let it actually boil. Stir into the mayonnaise mixture, making sure it is evenly distributed. Pour into a rinsed mold, or a pretty glass dish if you don't want to unmold. Chill well until set.

Unmold or not, and serve as a first course with brown bread and butter or fingers of watercress sandwiches.

JP

CERVEACH OF SOLE

Not to be confused with the South American *ceviche*, this old way of dressing fish requires the fish to be cooked first. I demonstrated it at a Georgian cooking forum, and thereafter found I was being served it all over Edinburgh. Do try it.

4 fillets of sole

oil

salt and freshly ground pepper

1 onion, sliced into thin rings

FOR THE DRESSING:

½ cup olive oil

2 tablespoons white wine vinegar

shredded zest and juice of 1 lemon

2 bayleaves

fresh herbs

Heat a film of cooking oil in a frying pan. Flatten each fish fillet with a rolling pin. Sprinkle on some salt and pepper and fold in half. Fry gently and briefly on both sides.

Arrange the fish on a long dish and scatter the onion rings over the top. Mix the dressing ingredients together and pour over the fish while it is still hot. Leave for at least 3 hours to cool. Serve at room temperature, garnished with the fresh herbs.

CDW

HALIBUT IN CIDER

This is a good summer dish. Halibut is a very under-used fish. Don't let your fishmonger cut the steaks too thin, and be sure to use dry alcoholic cider.

1½ cups chopped onions

2 tablespoons olive oil

1 garlic clove, minced

2½ cups hard apple cider

salt and freshly ground pepper

4 halibut steaks

2 lemons

1 pound ripe tomatoes, peeled and sliced

a handful of minced parsley

butter

Sauté the onions gently in the oil till pale gold. Add the garlic and cook a little longer. Stir in the cider, and add salt and pepper to taste.

Put the halibut steaks in a greased baking dish, season, and add the juice of 1 lemon. Thinly slice the remaining lemon and arrange over the fish. Pour the onions and cider over the fish. Place the tomatoes and minced parsley on top and dot with butter.

Bake in a preheated oven at 350°F for 20 minutes. Serve hot.

CDW

Clarissa's tip

Support your local fishmonger (if you are lucky enough to have a real one). Supermarket fish is revolting and never as fresh as it should be.

MEAT AND POULTRY

Outside the shop of butcher Jesse Smith in Cirencester, "A carnivore's delight"

CLARISSA WRITES: In this year of grace 1996, meat is a very important issue. More and more, the media are attacking the nutritional quality of meat without spelling out the actualities of the situation. Consequently the wrong people suffer. Butchers' meat, or indeed meat from the better supermarkets, is unlikely to be harmful. Setting aside the totally unproved, and in any event, fairly minor issue of Creutzfeldt Jakob disease, what is most likely to be unsafe is the scrapings of meat used in cheap burgers and made-up dishes. I suspect when the last trump comes, the single most destructive dish of the twentieth century will prove to be the hamburger, destructive to health, palate, and general enjoyment of food. Jennifer's comment on this type of meat is, "If you can't cut it from the carcass with a knife it isn't edible." To which I can only reply, "So wise, dear."

The other threat to the meat industry is the rise of the vegetarian. The Royal Society of Chemistry assesses that we need to eat meat at least twice a year to keep our amino acid levels up, and that in Third World societies with a vegetarian diet, sufficient animal protein is obtained from the weevils and rodent droppings in the stored starch and proteins (not something you'd find in supermarkets, alas!).

Jennifer and Clarissa prepare to cook in the kitchen of Westonbirt school

Not content with watching from the sidelines, Clarissa kits up to join the Westonbirt lacrosse team in goal

Jennifer reminisces

*W*hen I saw the job advertised – a live-in cook needed for a large central London apartment used by visiting dignitaries – I thought it sounded perfect. The visits were occasional, so most of the time I had the place to myself. It was huge, with cupboards full of Wedgewood china and the most ghastly furniture you've ever seen. It was perfect for parties.

They were always late for dinner, so meat stews that could sit and wait without spoiling were often on the menu. One day I thought I'd make a goulash and instead of dipping the meat in paprika, I mistakenly used cayenne instead, knowing they loved hot, spicy food. It was rather too hot – they nearly died.

I left a year later. One person thought it was perfectly acceptable to bring tarts home. I disagreed and told him so firmly and loudly. I was sacked for deep discourtesy.

Historically, most Empires turn to a meatless diet once their days in the sun are over, so I daresay we are just following suit.

When I talk to Jennifer about meat, her eyes go dreamy and she yearns for roasted marrow bones wrapped in a napkin, served with a silver marrow scoop and hot toast to put the marrow on, or for sweetbreads daintily served. My own yearnings are for rare barrons of beef or kidneys cooked in their own caul of fat, but I think you will find our recipes suitable to your own tables.

When it comes to meat, Jennifer and Clarissa are deadly serious

As I write, the venue for the program is reduced to a shortlist of two. We are making the program at a school, and curiously – and not of our doing – the two remaining on the short list are my alma mater and the director's. It would be strange to go back and cook at a place that tried so hard to ruin my appreciation of food, so I hope we choose the director's old school.

We seem to have included recipes for poultry in this section – because the book matches the series, there is no place else to put them. Don't regard this as any diminution of poultry. We both love it.

I think both Jennifer and I agree that with meat of any kind the trick is to buy the best you can afford. Don't waste good money on cheap steak, which may not be well aged, when for the same or less money you can get a beautiful piece of beef that will taste much better. Again, make friends with your butcher – he will tell you what is good. There have been periods of my life when I have been incredibly poor, and I have been amazed to discover how little one pays for the cheaper cuts and how much better some of them taste.

In Scotland, even the supermarkets sell soup bones and smoked ham bones for very little, as most people make their own soup. A few ham bones, an offcut, and some dried beans, and you can have a meal to serve to anyone.

Not something you see every day: Ron Tanner, a shepherd from Nesley Farm, encounters the ladies in a lane. Ron's tip for successful flock control: "To be a good shepherd, you've got to think like a sheep."

BEEF À LA WILL MORELAND

I have a friend who is almost as talented a cook as he is a violinist, and I am most grateful to him for this recipe.

2-pound piece of beef tenderloin
or boneless sirloin roast

2 tablespoons oil

1 bunch of scallions, minced

2 garlic cloves, minced

a piece of fresh ginger root the
size of your thumb, minced

1 tablespoon soy sauce

1 large bunch of fresh cilantro,
chopped

2 hot chili peppers, chopped

1 piece of fresh lemon grass,
roughly chopped

2 cans coconut milk

juice of 1 lime

Heat a heavy frying pan and sear your piece of meat thoroughly; remove. Heat the oil in the same pan and sauté the scallions, garlic, and ginger until softened. Add the soy sauce, half of the cilantro, and the chilies. The heat of the chilies is a matter of choice – you can use a Scots bonnet for ultra-hot or a seeded jalapeño for mild. Decide before you buy.

Place the seared meat in a roasting pan. Pour the fried vegetable mixture over. Add the lemon grass and pour the coconut milk and lime juice over the meat. Cook in a preheated oven at 350°F for 40 minutes.

Place the beef on a serving dish. Strain the sauce, add the rest of the minced cilantro and pour over the meat. Serve immediately.

CDW

Clarissa's tip

Make friends with your butcher, not just for good meat –
he'll also sharpen your knives.

ROAST RIB OF BEEF WITH SHALLOTS AND RASPBERRY VINEGAR

This is a great festive roast for a treat or a party.

8- to 10-pound beef rib roast

salt and freshly ground pepper

1 pound shallots, thinly sliced

butter

1 tablespoon raspberry vinegar

1 bottle of full-bodied red wine

Get your butcher to remove the rib bones, sinews, and backstrap from the meat, and have it tied into a roll. Keep the bones, and place them on the bottom of a roasting pan with the beef sitting on top. Season very well with salt and pepper. Roast in a preheated oven at 350–375°F, allowing 15 minutes to each pound, plus an extra 15 minutes for really rare meat (more time can, of course, be added to suit your taste). After cooking, let it rest on top of the stove for at least 15 minutes.

Meanwhile, cook the shallots in a little butter until lightly browned. Add the vinegar and two-thirds of the wine. Stew this brew with the lid off until it has reduced by half.

When you remove the meat and bones from the roasting pan, deglaze the pan with the remainder of the wine. Add any juices from the meat while it has been resting on some great warmed charger. Strain into the shallot and wine mixture and season to taste.

Serve thick slices of the roast covered with the sauce, with crisp roasted potatoes, broccoli or green beans, and buttered carrots. Magnificent.

JP

EEF WITH ANCHOVIES

In the Middle Ages, saltfish was cooked with meat, as it still is in the Caribbean. Anchovies were the great fashion in the Georgian Age, so this is their adaptation of the earlier idea.

10 anchovy fillets

2 tablespoons butter

a 2-pound rolled beef rib roast

2 carrots

1 onion

2 celery stalks

2 cups beef stock

Mash half of the anchovies with the butter. Melt in a pan and brown the beef in it. Remove the meat and discard the butter. Using a larding needle or a sharp knife, make small holes in the meat and insert the remaining anchovies.

Mince the carrots, onion, and celery and combine to make a *mirepoix*. Place the *mirepoix* of vegetables on the bottom of a heavy pan or Dutch oven. Put the beef on top and pour the stock over. Bring to a boil, then cook gently for 1½ hours, uncovered. Cut into slices for serving.

Clarissa's tip

Remember, the brighter the meat, the less it has been aged.

*R*OAST MEAT LOAF OR "HEDGEHOG"

I evolved this robust, strongly flavored monster when I had to feed a lot of people at a curious school in Padworth. It is excellent for picnics, parties, and christenings, let alone wakes.

½ pound good mushrooms, sliced

butter

salt and freshly ground pepper

grated nutmeg

½ pound chicken or turkey livers

1 pound each ground beef, ground pork, and ground veal or turkey

1 pound pork sausage meat

1 large onion, grated

3 fat garlic cloves, minced to a paste

10 juniper berries, crushed

1 heaping teaspoon ground allspice

sprigs of fresh thyme

1–2 eggs

½ pound sliced bacon

bayleaves

branches of fresh rosemary

Sauté the mushrooms in butter until the juices run, then season with salt and pepper plus a good grating of nutmeg. Reserve. Remove the sinews from the livers and slice. In a large bowl combine all the ground meats, the sausage meat, the livers, the onion, garlic, and juniper berries. Add the allspice and some thyme leaves. Season with salt and about 20 turns of the pepper mill. Beat the egg(s) and add to the mixture along with the sautéed mushrooms. Use your spotless hands to mix this whole lot together most thoroughly.

Oil a roasting pan and place all the mixture in it, molding it into an oval shape. Adorn with the slices of bacon, criss-crossed Union Jack-style, tucking the ends under the meat loaf. Strew some bayleaves and branches of rosemary on the top and sides. Cook in a preheated oven at 450°F for 15 minutes, then lower the heat to 350°F and cook for a further 1½ hours.

When cooked, there will be lots of lovely juices in the bottom of the pan; save them for flavoring soup, stock, or an egg dish. Remove the loaf and place on a good dish. Serve hot or cold with a tomato sauce made from fresh or canned tomatoes in the Italian manner.

For children, you might like to turn it into a "hedgehog" by pressing almonds into the meat to create prickles and placing 3 olives at one end to form eyes and a nose. This should be done before putting into the oven.

JP

COLLARED BEEF

This is a very good dish served cold, for a buffet. It can also be served hot with a dill or horseradish sauce. Collared beef is so called because it is served in the shape of a collar.

a 2- to 4-pound piece of flank steak or boned beef rib roast

2 tablespoons minced parsley

½ teaspoons each minced fresh sage, dried thyme, cayenne, and grated nutmeg or ground allspice

salt and freshly ground pepper

Remove any gristle from the meat. Mix together all the herbs and spices. Coat the inside of the meat with the mixture, roll up tightly, and tie with string. Wrap in a cloth, preferably cheesecloth.

Set the beef in a saucepan, cover with cold water, and bring to a boil. Reduce the heat and simmer one half hour for each pound.

Remove the beef from the pan. Put a heavy weight on the meat, without removing the cloth, and press until cooled. The best way to do this is to put a board over the meat and load it with weights or cans of food.

To serve, unwrap the meat and slice it thinly.

CDW

PORK TENDERLOIN IN PASTRY

This is a fine and beautiful dish to set before your friends, let alone a king.

FOR THE PASTRY:

1¾ cups flour

½ teaspoon salt

Make the pastry a day in advance. Sift the flour and salt into a bowl. Melt the butter very, very gently until liquid but not warm (if warm it hardens the dough). Mix into the flour with the other ingredients using a rubber spatula until all is smooth. Refrigerate for at least 30 minutes.

½ cup (1 stick) butter

1 cup sour cream

½ tablespoon white wine vinegar or brandy

1-pound pork tenderloin

dry mustard

salt and freshly ground pepper

butter and oil

several large handfuls of fresh green herbs (thyme, parsley, chives, tarragon, chervil, etc.)

1 large garlic clove, minced

½ cup whole milk

½ cup light cream

1 pound pork sausage meat

1½ cups fresh white bread crumbs

4–6 slices of cooked ham

1 egg and a little milk for egg wash

Divide the dough into 3 equal parts. Roll each piece out on a floured board until as thin as possible, then place them neatly on top of each other. Fold into three as you would a letter. Turn the pastry and fold again the other way. Wrap in wax paper and a cloth. Refrigerate.

Rub the pork tenderloin with mustard, salt, and pepper. Fry briskly in butter with a drop of oil, browning rapidly all over. Remove from the heat. Process any herbs you are using (watercress and spinach leaves can be used as well) with the garlic, milk, and the cream to form a purée. Mix with the sausage meat in a bowl. Add the bread crumbs and season to taste. The sausage meat mixture should be bright green, so do not stint on the herbs.

Roll out the pastry to an oblong that is 1 inch longer than the tenderloin and about three times as wide. Spread the sausage meat mixture over the dough, leaving a margin of 1 inch all around. Lay the sliced ham on top. Place the tenderloin in the middle and wrap the pastry around it to form a parcel. Moisten the lap-overs with egg wash and press the ends firmly together to seal. Turn onto an oiled baking sheet so the seam is on the bottom. Paint with egg wash all over and pierce with a sharp knife in several places to allow any steam to escape. Paint again with the egg wash. Bake in a preheated oven at 375°F for about 45 minutes.

When ready, remove from the oven and let it rest for 10 minutes before carving into fairly thick slices.

JP

ORK STROGANOFF

This is a steal from the famous Russian dish. I have used gin in the sauce, as I usually do with pork – the juniper flavor of gin goes admirably with the meat. The alcohol content evaporates so it can be served at the most temperate of gatherings.

a 1¾-pound pork tenderloin (approx.)

1 tablespoon olive oil

2 tablespoons butter

2 onions, thinly sliced

½ pound mushrooms, thinly sliced

salt and freshly ground black pepper

2 tablespoons gin

1¼ cups sour cream

minced parsley

paprika

Remove any unsightly fat or outer skin from the pork. Slice across the grain into rounds about ¼ inch thick. Heat half the oil and butter in a large frying pan until sizzling. Fry half the pork briskly to brown on both sides, about 3 minutes. Transfer to a plate with a slotted spoon. Cook the other half of the pork the same way.

Add the rest of the butter and oil to the pan and cook the onions gently until soft, then add the mushrooms and continue to cook gently, turning them over and over until the juices run. Season with a little salt and lots of pepper. Remove the pan contents to another plate.

Reinstate the pork rounds in the pan, heat gently, and pour the gin over the meat. Let it warm up for 2 minutes, then set fire to it and baste until the flames die out. Add the onions and mushrooms, stir in the sour cream, and bring to a bubbling simmer. Check seasoning.

Sprinkle with minced parsley and a goodly pinch of paprika. Serve immediately with buttered noodles or plain boiled rice.

JP

POT-ROASTED PORK WITH CARAWAY

This is another Elizabethan recipe. In Scotland, where I now live, loin of pork is not sold with its crackling (skin), so I have found myself looking for recipes for other cuts. Shoulder is good and cheaper than loin.

2 tablespoons oil or lard

a 4-pound boned pork shoulder roast

2 onions, sliced

2 tablespoons caraway seeds

4 apples (tart ones), sliced

salt and freshly ground pepper

6 dates, pitted and halved

1 piece of candied citrus peel, minced

1 bunch of celery, minced

grated zest and juice of 1 orange

a sprig of fresh sage

½ bottle of red wine

beef stock

Heat the oil or lard in a frying pan and brown the pork roast over a high heat, turning to color all sides. Remove. Fry the onions in the same fat to a light brown. Add the caraway seeds and cook until they start to pop.

Put the onion and caraway mixture into a deep baking dish or casserole. Layer the sliced apples on top. Season the pork and place on this mixture. Add the dates, candied peel, celery, orange zest, and sage. Pour on the wine and orange juice and add enough stock to come to the top of but not cover the meat. Cook in a preheated oven at 325°F for 2½ hours.

Remove the meat. Strain the cooking liquid and remove the fat from the surface. Serve the liquid as a sauce.

CDW

Clarissa's tip

If you do want good crackling on pork, you could do a lot worse than to take a leaf out of Fanny Craddock's book and "rub salt into the skin as if into the face of your worst enemy."

ROAST SHOULDER OF LAMB STUFFED WITH FIG BALLS

I discovered fig balls at that wonderful emporium Valvonna and Crolla, in Edinburgh, described by Elizabeth David as the best Italian food shop in Great Britain. I assure you, nothing's changed. Fig balls are traditional for Christmas in Italy. The figs are formed into balls and roasted slowly, then wrapped in grape leaves. I buy a whole lot at Christmas to last me. The taste and texture is rich and sensuous. If you can't find fig balls, you can use dried figs resuscitated in cold tea, but they are not as good.

1 shoulder of lamb

1–2 fig balls
(depending on size of roast)

1 onion, minced

salt and freshly ground pepper

a wineglass (4–5fl oz) of port

Bone the lamb shoulder (or have your butcher do it for you).

Break up the fig balls and mix with the onion. Season with salt and pepper. Stuff the lamb with this and sew up or secure with skewers. Roast in a preheated oven at 350°F for 15 minutes per pound.

Remove the roast from the pan and set it aside to rest while you deglaze the roasting juices with the port. Reduce to make a sauce and check the seasoning. Serve with the lamb.

CDW

ANCASHIRE HOTPOT

Whenever I read Dorothy Hartley's great book, *Food in England,* I become enraged by how deprived we are today to lose so much of our local identity. How far removed are mushy hamburgers, which are possibly poisoning us, from the old local dishes and local breeds of animal. This dish was designed specially for the long-boned sheep of the Pennines, but I doubt you will find their long-tailed chops today. Ideally it should be made with mutton, which has so much more flavor than lamb, but I expect you will have to make do with middle-aged hogget. Still, it is not a bad dish. A nice touch is to place a dozen fresh oysters under the potatoes.

8 mutton or lamb chops with their tail bones

flour

salt and freshly ground pepper

drippings or oil

4 lamb kidneys

4 onions, sliced

4 carrots, sliced

3–4 potatoes, thickly sliced

1 teaspoon sugar

Trim the fat from your chops, dredge with flour, and season. Fry them in hot drippings or oil till brown on both sides. Stand them vertically in a long casserole with the bones pointing upward. Throw in the kidneys. Fry the onions lightly and pack among the chops, alternating with layers of sliced carrots.

Arrange the potato slices on top, overlapping them to form a roof. Pour off the fat from the frying pan and make a gravy with a sprinkling of flour and about 2 cups of boiling water. Season and add the sugar. Pour into the casserole (the gravy should come about two-thirds of the way up the meat), cover, and cook in a preheated oven at 350°F for 2 hours.

About 10 minutes before serving, remove the lid and allow the potatoes to brown. This dish is particularly good if made the day before and allowed to cool so that any surplus fat can be removed.

CDW

HAM WITH LEEKS AND CREAM SAUCE

This is a very useful concoction if you are expecting a lot of people for dinner. It looks and tastes splendid, but the great thing is you can prepare it the day before, then just bung it in the oven when required.

SERVES 8–10

a 3- to 4-pound uncooked ham

2 pounds leeks

6 tablespoons butter,
plus extra for the top

3 tablespoon flour

2½ cups milk, warmed

1 cup dry vermouth, warmed

salt and freshly ground pepper

1 cup heavy cream

½ cup grated Gruyère cheese

Place the ham in a snug saucepan and cover completely with cold water. Bring slowly to the simmering point and cook at a bare tremble for half an hour to each pound, timing from the moment you put it on to cook. Remove from the heat and let it rest for a further half hour in its water. Turn out into a clean sink to peel off any rind. Meanwhile, be getting on with the sauce.

Slice the washed and trimmed leeks finely, using the slicing device of a food processor or a good, sharp knife. Melt the butter in a large saucepan and stew the leeks until tender. Add the flour and stir until well mixed with the leeks. Add the warm milk, little by little, together with the warm vermouth, stirring all the time to make a smooth sauce. Season with a generous amount of freshly ground black pepper and very little salt. Simmer very gently for 20–30 minutes, stirring occasionally. Use a flame diffuser if available. Add the cream and the cheese, mixing well until the cheese has melted. Check the seasoning, remembering the ham will be salty.

Carve the ham into thickish slices. Pour half the sauce into a good earthenware baking dish. Arrange the ham in overlapping slices on the sauce, then cover with the remaining sauce. Dot with tiny bits of butter and heat in a preheated 350°F oven for 10 minutes. Finish off under the broiler until the top is brown and bubbly.

Serve with some simple new potatoes and something bright green, like spinach or broccoli. This is also a good way to use leftover ham, with half or a quarter of the amount of sauce.

JP

A.N.'S *S*LOW SHOULDER OF LAMB

My beloved A.N. Wilson dreamt up this dish for the hurried cook who has to go out and about and likes to return to a *fait accompli* at the end of the day. He is a very good cook and deeply interested in food, but has little time to indulge. This receipt uses cans of beans but you can, of course, cook your own if you prefer.

1 lamb shoulder roast, about 4 pounds

2 large (14oz) cans of cannellini beans or 4 small (7oz) ones

1¼–2 cups white wine

2 large onions, roughly chopped

10 shallots, roughly chopped

6 tomatoes, quartered

3 tablespoons tomato paste

10 whole garlic cloves, peeled

salt and black peppercorns

2 bayleaves

3 branches of fresh rosemary

Ask your butcher to cut off the shank end of the shoulder but keep it. (This makes it easier to fit in a casserole.) Put both pieces of the shoulder in a good casserole. Cover with the beans and their liquid, the wine, onions and shallots, the tomatoes and the paste, the garlic, several crushed peppercorns and salt to taste. Tuck in the bayleaves and the rosemary. A.N. has an Aga and cooks the shoulder for about 4 hours in the simmering oven and then in the roasting oven for another hour or so to suit himself. With an ordinary range, I would put the covered casserole in a preheated oven at 275°F for the 4 hours, then increase the temperature to 425°F for the last part. Have a look at it now and then to make sure it is not drying out; also give it the odd stir to combine all the vegetables and juices.

The first 4 hours can be done the day before and is really no trouble. I would also add some anchovies, which are excellent with lamb; you cannot actually taste them, but they have a very enhancing effect on the flavor. Black olives are another good addition. At the end of cooking, the meat will drop off the bone and all the fat will have disappeared into the vegetables in some miraculous manner. Serve in big old-fashioned soup plates. For accompaniment this dish requires nothing more than a vast, crisp green salad and a good crust of bread.

JP

REAL SCOTCH EGGS

This is a very different object from those revolting things to be found in British pubs and on supermarket shelves.

MAKES 10

10 extra large eggs

½ pound cooked ham

6 anchovy fillets

2½ cups fresh bread crumbs

½ teaspoon apple-pie spice

freshly ground black pepper

bacon drippings or butter and a little oil

Beat 2 of the eggs in a shallow bowl. Put the other 8 eggs into a saucepan of cold water, bring to a boil, and simmer for 5 minutes. Plunge into cold water and peel. This method should produce a slightly softer yolk than rock hard, which I think is nicer.

Process, grind, or mince the ham and anchovies. Combine with the bread crumbs, spice, some black pepper, and most of the beaten egg. Brush each boiled egg with the remaining beaten egg and encase with the ham mixture, molding it around the egg with your hands.

Fry in the bacon drippings or butter with the addition of a slug of olive oil until brown all over. Cut in half and serve on fried bread or toast. Eaten with a crisp, green salad and a glass of wine, this makes an excellent little luncheon dish.

JP

STOVED HOWTOWDIE WITH DRAPPIT EGGS

I love the name of this recipe. Since I moved to Scotland, my friend June Bertram, from Whitecraig, has been teaching me to speak properly. I'm "away the messages" when I go for my shopping, and I'll see you the "morns morn" or the "morns nicht." It's all verra confusin, ye ken. A howtowdie is a young hen of about 2 pounds, and to stove it, from the French *estuvier*, is to cook it enclosed. Drappit eggs are poached eggs because they are drappit in the water, i.e. dropped in the water. Kale is traditionally served with this, but you can substitute spinach.

a 2-pound chicken

salt and freshly ground pepper

FOR THE HERB STUFFING:

1–2 onions, minced

1–2 garlic cloves, minced

butter

2¼ cups fresh bread crumbs

lots of fresh green herbs, chopped

4 tablespoons butter

½ pound shallots, chopped

1 bouquet garni

½ teaspoon dried rosemary

2 cups chicken stock

4 eggs

Season the chicken inside and out. Make the stuffing by softening the onions and garlic in butter, then adding the bread crumbs and herbs and frying gently until golden. Stuff the chicken.

Melt the butter in a Dutch oven and brown the chicken all over. Add the shallots, bouquet garni, and rosemary. Pour the stock over. Cover tightly and simmer for 1 hour until the chicken is tender. Remove the chicken from the stock and keep warm.

Ladle some of the cooking liquid into another pan and poach the eggs in this. The rest of the stock can be used to make soup.

To serve, place flattened balls of kale or spinach on a flat serving dish. Place the poached eggs on top of these and put the chicken in the center.

CDW

POUSSIN WITH GARLIC

I first made this dish with smoked garlic, which I found in my local market; however, it is not readily available, so use the natural. A good mixture of tastes from the four corners of the earth.

2 poussins or squab chickens, 1½ pounds each

black olive paste (tapenade)

lemon juice

6 tablespoons olive oil

10 plump garlic cloves

⅔ cup dry vermouth

sea salt and freshly ground pepper

bayleaves

Chinese brown bean sauce

Take a small Dutch oven that will hold the birds snugly. Put a tablespoon of olive paste and a good squeeze of lemon into each cavity. Heat the olive oil in the Dutch oven and brown the poussins all over, turning from side to side. Add the peeled cloves of garlic and allow to cook gently for a minute or two. Pour in the vermouth. Season well with salt and pepper, and tuck in a couple of bayleaves. Brush the birds liberally with some bean sauce.

Cover the Dutch oven with its lid and cook in a preheated oven at 375°F for about 45 minutes until tender. Baste every 15 minutes.

Good served with rice.

JP

DUCK IN HONEY SAUCE

I remember my mother cooking duck, which she rubbed enthusiastically with salt and honey. The duck was so good that Boris Chaliapin, the son of the great opera singer, espying one left over at the end of the lunch, devoured the lot by way of a snack. For my mother's method, roast at 350°F for 2 hours. This is a variant on the idea.

4 duck breasts

½ cup (1 stick) butter

2 tablespoons olive oil

1 onion, minced

6 tablespoons white wine

¼ cup honey

2 sprigs of fresh thyme

juice of 1 lemon

2 cups heavy cream

salt and freshly ground pepper

Cut each duck breast into two. Heat 4 tablespoons butter with the oil in a frying pan and fry the pieces of duck without allowing them to color. Add the onion and allow to soften. Remove the duck from the pan and keep warm. Pour off any excess fat.

Add the wine to the pan and boil to reduce slightly. Stir in the honey and thyme. Add the lemon juice and cream, and season with salt and pepper. Replace the duck in the pan; cover and cook for a further 5 minutes.

Remove the duck to a serving dish. Discard the thyme and swirl the remaining butter, in small pieces, into the sauce. Pour the sauce over the duck and garnish with fresh thyme.

CDW

HONEY-GLAZED DUCK WITH GINGER AND PINK GRAPEFRUIT

Eton College put on a Jennifer Paterson evening – I was invited to dinner and they cooked my recipes for me, including this one. The sauce can be made the day before.

FOR THE SAUCE:

3 pink grapefruit

¼ cup sugar

2 tablespoons honey

2 tablespoons dark soy sauce

juice of 1 lemon

2 teaspoons freshly grated ginger root

1 tablespoon cornstarch

2 tablespoons water

salt and freshly ground pepper

4–5 boneless duck breasts

1 tablespoon clear honey

1 tablespoon dark soy sauce

Make the sauce first. Peel the grapefruit with a very sharp, stainless steel knife, working over a bowl to catch all the juice. Remove all pith and cut the sections from their skin. Squeeze the juice from all the pith and skin, which should amount to 1¼ cups. Place the sugar in a dry saucepan over a gentle heat. When it begins to melt, stir until it is caramelized. It will start to bubble and rise in the pan. Remove from the heat and continue stirring until it subsides. Pour in the grapefruit juice at arm's length, as it may splatter alarmingly. Return to the heat and add the honey, soy sauce, lemon juice, and grated ginger. Stir until simmering and the caramel has dissolved. Blend the cornstarch and the water to form a smooth paste, and gradually stir into the sauce until it becomes thick and clear. Add a good grinding of black pepper and salt to taste. Finally, add the grapefruit sections. Remove from the heat.

Prick the duck's skin all over. Place the breasts skin-side up on a rack in a roasting pan, with a little water in the bottom. Mix the honey and the soy sauce together and brush over the skins. Cook in a preheated oven at 400°F for 30 minutes until the skin is crisp.

Remove from the rack and carve the breasts diagonally into ¼-inch slices. Arrange on a fine warmed platter and pour the heated sauce over the duck. Serve with nice little potatoes, baby carrots, and peas.

JP

CHICKEN TAGINE WITH CARDOONS

In 1989, I began my campaign to restore that wonderful vegetable, the cardoon, to our hearts and homes. It is unlikely that I have succeeded, but I do know that when people come into the shop they frequently greet me with "Ah, you're the Cardoon Lady." I do not object. *Tagines* are native to Morocco and are an excellent and succulent way of cooking (the name is used both for the earthenware pot, with conical lid, and the stew cooked inside it).

2 pounds cardoons

a 3-pound chicken, boned and cut into chunks

2 garlic cloves, minced

1 teaspoon ground ginger

¼ teaspoon turmeric

2 tablespoons chopped fresh cilantro

2 onions, grated

oil

salt and freshly ground pepper

2 preserved lemons, rinsed and quartered

¾ cup Kalamata olives, rinsed and pitted

½ cup lemon juice

Trim and de-string the cardoons. Cut into 3-inch pieces. Keep in acidulated water to prevent discoloration.

In a *tagine* or Dutch oven, combine the chunks of chicken, the garlic, spices, cilantro, onions, some oil, and some salt. Cover with 1¼ cups of water and bring to a boil. Reduce the heat and simmer for 1 hour.

Add the cardoons and enough fresh water to cover them (there should be enough liquid to cover them for the first 20 minutes of cooking). Continue cooking for 40 minutes in all. Add the preserved lemons, olives, and lemon juice for the last 10 minutes of cooking.

Strain off the cooking liquid and reduce to a thick gravy. Pour back over the chicken. Lest you are confused, the total cooking time is 1 hour and 40 minutes.

CDW

CHICKEN BREASTS WITH WALNUT AILLADE

In the fascinating book *Goose Fat and Garlic*, Jean and Paul Strang give this *aillade* recipe. Every time they came to do a demonstration and book-signing for me, they made up a batch. I was so addicted to it, I used to ask them to make double so I could take it home. Here is one of the things I did with it.

½ cup walnut pieces

cloves from a large garlic bulb, peeled

salt and freshly ground pepper

⅔ cup walnut oil

a handful of minced parsley

1 chicken breast half per person

1¼ cups plain yogurt (approx.)

lemon juice

peanut or other cooking oil

In a food processor, grind the walnuts and garlic as finely as you can. Add 1 tablespoon cold water to help the amalgamation. Season with salt and pepper, and slowly blend in the oil until you have a thick sauce almost like a mayonnaise. Stir in the parsley.

Marinate the chicken breasts in the yogurt, seasoned with salt, pepper, and a little lemon juice, for half an hour. Wipe off surplus yogurt.

Heat some oil in a frying pan and pan-fry the chicken for about 3 minutes each side to sear. Spoon over the *aillade* and cook over a low heat until the chicken is done, about 12–15 minutes.

CDW

Illustrated overleaf

CAKES AND BAKING

CLARISSA WRITES: I can still remember the day in 1983, at the age of 36, when I obtained a new cooking job I very much wanted. As I was leaving the interview, my new boss remarked quite casually: "Oh, and we always like to have a cake or two knocking about." I dashed in panic to my greatest friend, saying, "I can't take the job, I've never baked a cake in my life" (that wasn't true – I did when I was 11, and invented the Frisbee!). As so often before, she convinced me to try, and I spent a week in her house learning to bake. I went on to win a prize in a competition organized by that SAS of British cookery, the Women's Institute... The moral of this story is to reassure you that anyone can learn if they are willing or desperate enough. True *pâtissières* are born, not made: they have ice water in the veins of their hands, are thin and nervous from the strains of perfection, and carry kitchen scales with their cooking equipment. I am not one of their number, but I get real pleasure from baking and I have learned certain things.

Jennifer and Clarissa sample the wares at the Baines Tea Rooms in Uppingham

While other cookery has room for error and a freehand style, it is important to measure carefully in baking... to be thorough in your folding, creaming, and measuring... and to line your baking pans carefully and butter them, when directed, as thoroughly as *Last Tango in Paris*. It is also important to remember, for your own

68

self-worth, that even the most experienced bakers have off days, and that fruit inexplicably sinks in fruit cakes.

In this program Jennifer and I will be venturing forth into that well-loved British Institution, the village fête. At the time of writing, it is too early to tell you where or what, as our fearless researchers are at present scouring the wilds of Britain for virginal (in the TV sense) villages and lovely goods.

When I talk to Jennifer about this program she waxes eloquent on scones – she has Scottish origins, and no doubt her race memory reminds her that North of the Border the test of a woman's mettle is her ability with a scone (it is true that there are some pretty awful specimens about). I keep thinking of my mother, who made wonderful pastry. She had been told that it was vital to keep your hands cold when making pastry. Consequently, in winter it was unwise to go into the kitchen, as every window was open and a huge bowl of ice water stood beside her for her to plunge her hands into. One had to send for mountain rescue to thaw her out when she had finished.

Sweet baking is always done with unsalted butter, and most good bakers use all-purpose flour and add their own quantity of baking powder. There are endless theories about which flour strength to use. I tend to use bread flour for bread, all-purpose flour for pastry, and self-rising flour for cakes.

Finally, don't forget that failures can always be turned into something else. There is a brilliant book called *Loaf, Crust and Crumb* by Silvija Davidson. The first part of the book is a dictionary of breads and the second is recipes for using up left-over bread. I do recommend it.

Jennifer prepares to demonstrate the art of baking

YORKSHIRE GINGERBREAD

Anne Willan, of La Varenne Cookery School, hails from North Allerton in North Yorkshire, and this is her gingerbread recipe, taken from her splendid compilation *Real Food*.

1⅔ cups self-rising flour

2 tablespoons ground ginger

1 tablespoon ground allspice

½ teaspoon salt

1 teaspoon baking soda

½ cup (1 stick) unsalted butter

½ cup packed dark brown sugar

3 eggs, beaten

⅔ cup black treacle or molasses

Sift the flour, ginger, allspice, salt, and baking soda into a bowl. In another bowl, cream the butter and brown sugar until very soft. Beat in the eggs one by one, then mix in the treacle or molasses. Gently fold in the sifted dry ingredients.

Pour the mixture into a greased and parchment-lined 8-inch square cake pan and bake in a preheated oven at 325°F for 50–60 minutes, or until the top springs back when pressed.

Cool in the pan, then remove and store for a few days in an airtight tin before eating. The cake can be served in slices spread with butter, or with clotted cream and stem ginger in syrup.

CDW

Apple Jalousie

Everyone must make puff pastry at least once, so that they then have a choice whether to make it or buy it, so I have given a recipe here.

This dessert takes its name from the effect of *jalousies*, or blinds, that is created by the cooked pastry. The word comes from the Norman French *jallouse*, to look through. I like to think of those knights peering through the visors. It is an easy and delicious dish and a great standby of mine.

1 pound frozen puff pastry, thawed, or half the recipe of puff pastry

½ cup chunky marmalade

1 pound tart apples, peeled, cored, and sliced

egg white to glaze

sugar

Roll out the pastry to a 12-inch square. Cut in half and place one half on a greased baking sheet. Spread with the marmalade, leaving a 1-inch margin all around, then cover the marmalade with the sliced apples.

Roll the remaining piece of pastry to a 13- by 8-inch rectangle and fold in half lengthwise. Using a sharp knife, cut into the fold at ½-inch intervals, to within 1 inch of the edge and ends. Brush the pastry margin with water and position the lid over the apples, unfolding it to cover evenly. Fit the margins carefully together. Press all around with the flat of the knife, then scallop or flute the edges.

Brush with egg white and dredge evenly with sugar. Bake in a preheated oven at 425°F for 25–30 minutes until well risen and golden brown. This can be prepared before dinner and put in to bake during the main course.

CDW

UFF PASTRY

This pastry will keep for 3–6 months in the freezer.

1 pound (3¼ cups) flour

1 teaspoon salt

1 pound (4 sticks) unsalted butter

1¼ cups ice water

a squeeze of lemon juice

Sift the flour and salt into a large mixing bowl and rub in 6 tablespoons of the butter. Bind to a fairly soft dough with as much ice water as you need, adding the lemon juice too, and knead lightly. Roll out to a 12-inch square.

Form the remaining butter into an oblong block. It should be soft but firm. Place on one half of the pastry square and fold the pastry over to enclose it, sealing the edges with a rolling pin. Rib by pressing the rolling pin across the top at intervals.

Turn the pastry so that the fold is to the right, and roll out into a strip three times as long as wide. Fold the bottom third upward and the top third downward evenly. Seal the edges and chill in a plastic bag for 30 minutes.

Repeat this process five more times, always keeping the fold on the right. Chill overnight or for at least 1 hour before the final rolling. The pastry is now ready to use.

CDW

TILLYPRONIE ORANGE FOOL WITH ORANGE SHORTBREAD

Lady Clarke of Tillypronie wrote a wonderful cookery book in 1909. I once asked the late great Elizabeth David what was her favorite book and she replied "Lady Clarke's." Today I am honored to possess Elizabeth David's copy as a present from her family. It is well used and annotated in her familiar hand. Southover Press has produced a facsimile edition, and I do recommend it to you. I copy the orange fool exactly here – it is so easy and simple, and very, very good:

"Take a pint [2½ cups] of cream, beat 3 eggs well into it; and add the juice of 6 sweet oranges and the grated rind of a Seville orange; sugar to your taste and stir well over the fire till it thickens."

I cook it in a double boiler, then turn it out to cool, and serve with the shortbread.

Annie Bell's food is responsible for my career as a cookbook-seller. It is a long and complicated story, but suffice it to say that I ate her food enthusiastically every day for six months and could never fault it. If you remember that she is a vegetarian, which I very much am not, I can find no higher praise. Today she is a much-acclaimed food writer, and in her book, *Feast of Flavors*, she has transformed my old shortbread recipe with the addition of orange zest.

1 cup (2 sticks) butter

⅓ cup sugar

2 tablespoons vanilla-flavored sugar

1½ cups flour

finely grated zest of 3 oranges

1⅓ cups ground almonds

Put all the ingredients into a food processor and process to a dough. Wrap in plastic wrap and chill overnight.

Roll out to ½-inch thickness and cut into shapes. Transfer to a baking sheet. Leave to rest in the refrigerator for 1 hour.

Bake in a preheated oven at 275°F for 40 minutes or until golden. Remove to racks to cool. Store in airtight containers.

CDW

*A*DULT CHOCOLATE CAKE

Here is a cake to satisfy the chocoholics to the fill. I say cake, but it contains no flour and is more like a baked mousse with crispy sides. Whatever it is, it is outrageously rich and therefore highly recommendable.

8 ounces good bittersweet chocolate

1 cup (2 sticks) unsalted butter, softened

1½ cups sugar

5 eggs

Grease a cake pan 8¾ inches in diameter and 1½ inches deep (approximately).

Break the chocolate into a bowl large enough to receive all the other ingredients. Set over a saucepan of barely simmering water until melted. Remove from the heat and cool slightly. Cut the butter into little pieces and beat into the chocolate. Add the sugar and blend well, beating thoroughly. In another bowl, beat the eggs until very frothy and foamy, then gently fold into the chocolate mixture; make sure everything is thoroughly combined.

Pour the mixture into the cake pan and place it in a roasting pan containing enough water to come up 1 inch of the cake pan's side. Bake in a preheated oven at 350°F for 1 hour, then let it cool completely in the pan. When cold, remove from the water-filled pan and chill in the refrigerator overnight. Do not attempt to eat it while still warm. When ready to eat, run a metal spatula around the edge of the pan and, with a good thump, unmold the cake. Serve with whipped cream or ice cream. It's a killer.

JP

COFFEE MERINGUE

This is one of those delightful desserts that can be whipped up in a moment once you have a batch of meringues at your bidding. You can even use bought ones. As I always have many frozen egg whites waiting to be used up, I usually have a tin of meringues at the ready. To make meringues, which couldn't be easier, use 2 tablespoons superfine sugar to each egg white. Whisk the egg whites until really stiff, whisk in half the sugar until stiff again, and then fold in the rest of the sugar. Cover the baking sheet with parchment paper and dollop the meringue mixture in 2-teaspoon-size blobs over the surface as neatly as possible. Bake in a preheated oven at 240°F for 1½ hours. Leave to cool, then store in a large tin.

¾ cup blanched almonds

2 teaspoons sugar

8 meringues

1¼ cups heavy cream

2–3 tablespoons strong brewed coffee

freshly ground coffee

Chop up the almonds and heat with the sugar in a frying pan until brown and caramelized, turning them all the time as they can burn in a moment. Turn out to cool on some wax paper. Break up the meringues into a lovely glass bowl. Whip the cream until it stands in soft peaks, mix in the coffee, and spoon over the meringues. Scatter the sugared almonds over the whipped cream and, finally, sprinkle some freshly ground coffee over the lot.

Delicious, d'lovely, and delectable, and mostly made of air.

JP

LEMON MERINGUE ROULADE

With all the books in our shop, there is one food writer I know will never let me down when it comes to cakes, and that is Claire Macdonald. Since I moved to Scotland, Claire and her husband Godfrey, Lord Macdonald, have become my great friends. They own Kinloch Lodge Hotel on the Isle of Skye. Somehow the beauty of the "far Cuillins" is greatly enhanced with a plate of this delicious roulade.

5 egg whites

¾ cup superfine sugar

1 teaspoon cornstarch

confectioners' sugar

1¼ cups heavy cream

6 tablespoons lemon curd

Line the sides and bottom of a 12½- by 8½-inch jelly-roll pan with parchment paper. Whisk the egg whites until white, frothy, and doubled in bulk. Add 1 tablespoon superfine sugar and whisk until the egg whites are stiff but not too dry. The mixture should fall in soft peaks. Gradually whisk in half of the remaining superfine sugar, then continue to whisk until the meringue is very stiff and shiny. With a large metal spoon fold in the remaining superfine sugar and the cornstarch.

Spoon the meringue into the pan and level the surface. Bake in a preheated oven at 220°F for 45 minutes. Cool, uncovered, for 1 hour.

Unmold the meringue onto a sheet of parchment paper dusted with confectioners' sugar. Peel away the lining parchment from the base. Whip the cream until lightly thickened. Spread the cream over the meringue, then spread with lemon curd. Roll up the roulade from one of the short ends. Serve immediately, dusted with confectioners' sugar.

CDW

CHOPPED WALNUT AND COFFEE CAKE

I think this is a Polish receipt. I find it very excellent, not at all like an English cake. It has no flour, and its interesting texture and slightly bitter taste make it an elegant and very grown-up delicacy. Splendid with iced coffee on a sunny afternoon by the pool (dream away).

4 eggs

1 cup confectioners' sugar

1 tablespoon fine fresh bread crumbs

1 tablespoon finely ground fresh coffee

1 tablespoon unsweetened cocoa powder

1½ cups roughly minced walnuts

FOR THE FROSTING:

½ cup (1 stick) unsalted butter, softened

1 cup confectioners' sugar, sifted

1 egg yolk

1 tablespoon instant coffee powder

2 tablespoons boiling water

Grease and line (with parchment) a cake pan that is 8 inches in diameter and 2 inches deep.

Separate the yolks from the egg whites. Cream the yolks and sugar together until pale yellow and hanging like ribbons from the beater. Add the bread crumbs, ground coffee, cocoa, and walnuts and mix well together. Whisk the egg whites until stiff and carefully fold into the walnut mixture. Pour the batter into the prepared cake pan and bake in a preheated oven at 350°F for 45 minutes. Cool in the pan, then unmold onto a rack.

To make the frosting, cream the butter with the confectioners' sugar and egg yolk. Dissolve the instant coffee in the boiling water and mix well into the frosting. Spread over the cake with a wet knife.

JP

GALETTE DES ROIS AUX AMANDES (THE THREE KINGS ALMOND TART)

This cake is eaten on the feast of the Epiphany, the twelfth night after Christmas when the three kings arrived with their gifts for the Christ Child. A bean or a gold ring or even a tiny image of the Child is hidden in the cake and the top is surmounted with a golden cardboard crown. When the cake is eaten, the person who finds the object is crowned King of the Feast for the evening's festivities.

FOR THE PASTRY:

1¾ cups flour

½ teaspoon salt

½ cup + 6 tablespoons (1¾ sticks) unsalted butter

⅔ cup chilled water (approx.)

FOR THE FILLING:

½ cup (1 stick) unsalted butter

½ cup + 2 tablespoons sugar

3 egg yolks

4 drops of pure almond extract (not flavoring)

3 tablespoons kirsch or the like

1⅓ cups freshly ground almonds

1 dried bean, gold ring, or tiny baby figurine

confectioners' sugar

For the pastry, sift the flour and salt into a large bowl. Cut in 6 tablespoons of the butter with a sharp knife until the mixture resembles crumbs. Mix in just enough of the water to make a non-sticky dough. Knead gently, then cover and leave for 20 minutes.

Roll out the pastry on a floured board to about ¼-inch thickness. Dot it with one-third of the remaining butter cut into dice. Fold the pastry into three like a letter, then again into three in the opposite direction like a napkin. Cover with a cloth and refrigerate for 20 minutes. Repeat this process twice more, and leave for another 20 minutes' chilling before using. If you can't face all that fun, buy 1 pound frozen puff pastry instead.

Divide the pastry in half. Roll out each half into a round about 9 inches in diameter. Let them rest while you make the filling.

Cream the butter and sugar together until light and fluffy. Whisk in 2 of the egg yolks, the almond extract, kirsch, and the ground almonds. Work together until you have a smooth paste.

Rinse a baking sheet under cold water. Place one of the pastry rounds on the sheet and spoon the paste onto it, leaving a 2-inch margin all around. Hide the bean or the other objects in the paste. Beat the remaining egg with a little water and paint the pastry margin. Place the second round of pastry on top and gently press the edges together. Chill for 45 minutes.

Preheat the oven to 375°F. Using a sharp knife, make a lattice or star-shaped pattern on the pastry surface, but do not cut through to the filling. Pinch the edges prettily together. Paint the top with the egg wash. Bake the galette for 30–40 minutes until the pastry is crisp and brown. Transfer to a rack and cool. Dust with confectioners' sugar and broil for a minute, if desired.

When cool, serve with a gold crown on top (made with your own fair hands) and a glass of kirsch or some sweet dessert wine. Eat, and discover who will be King of the Feast, then crown him or her.

JP

DANISH APPLE AND PRUNE CAKE

This is a recipe from the great Australian cook Greta Anna. I hope you love it as much as I do. I had a Danish great-grandmother, but she couldn't cook, so thank you Greta Anna.

FOR THE BATTER:

½ cup + 2 tablespoons (1¼ sticks) butter

1 cup sugar

2 eggs, well beaten

½ cup + 2 tablespoons self-rising flour

1⅓ cups ground almonds

½ cup milk

1 teaspoon vanilla extract

1 tablespoon boiling water

½ teaspoon baking powder

FURTHER INGREDIENTS:

8 pitted prunes, minced

1 cup finely minced walnuts, mixed with 2 tablespoons sugar

2 green apples, cored and sliced

3 tablespoons sugar

ground cinnamon

butter

Cream together all the ingredients for the batter in a food processor, running it for 10 seconds. Run a spatula around the bowl and process for 5 more seconds. Pour into a well-buttered 10-inch round cake pan.

Place the prunes on the batter. Spoon the walnut and sugar mixture over. Arrange the apple slices on top of the walnuts. Bake in a preheated oven at 375°F for 45 minutes.

Sprinkle the surface with the sugar and some cinnamon. Dot with butter and bake for a further 20–25 minutes till a skewer comes out clean. Cool in the pan.

CDW

$\int$ODA BREAD

I love soda bread. It brings back memories of holidays in Ireland as a child, and my mother's tales of damper bread in Australia. I had forgotten about making it till I moved to Scotland, and watched my friend Marianne making it as easy as breathing.

2 cups whole-wheat flour

¾ cup self-rising flour

1 heaping teaspoon baking soda

salt

1 tablespoon margarine or butter

buttermilk

Sift the flours, baking soda, and salt to taste together into a bowl. Tip in the bran left in the sifter. Rub in the fat, then add enough buttermilk to make a dough.

Turn the dough onto a floured baking sheet and shape it into a round. Slash a deep cross in the top. Bake in a preheated oven at 400°F for 20–25 minutes. Put a large cake pan over the top to help it rise.

Wrap the bread in a clean cloth as you remove it from the oven, to prevent the crust from becoming too thick and hard.

CDW

ℬARM BRACK

This excellent fruit bread is associated with St. Brigid in Ireland, and is eaten there on her feast day, February 1st. In other places it was eaten at Halloween when there was a thimble, button, or silver coin lurking inside, or even a gold ring.

a 0.6-ounce cake fresh compressed yeast or a ¼-ounce envelope active dry yeast

½ teaspoon granulated sugar

1 tablespoon warm (105°F to 115°F) water

4 cups white bread flour

1 teaspoon salt

½ teaspoon each ground cinnamon and nutmeg

4 tablespoons butter

½ cup packed brown sugar

1 egg, beaten

1¼ cups warm (105°F to 115°F) milk

1 cup golden raisins

⅓ cup diced mixed candied citrus peel

milk and sugar to glaze

Blend the yeast with the granulated sugar, water, and ½ teaspoon of the flour. It is ready when it becomes frothy.

Sift the remaining flour into a bowl with the salt and spices. Rub in the butter, then add the brown sugar and make a well in the center. Pour in the yeast mixture, the beaten egg, and most of the milk. Mix into a dough and beat until it begins to leave the side of the bowl. Add the raisins and peel. Turn into a warmed, greased loaf pan, cover, and leave to rise for an hour or so, until almost double in size.

Preheat the oven to 400°F. Bake the brack for 10 minutes, then lower the heat to 350°F and bake for a further 45 minutes. Paint the top with a little milk and sugar, and return to the oven for a few minutes to glaze.

JP

Scones

Fresh scones, still warm from the oven, are part and parcel of the delicious teas of my childhood. No one seems to make them nowadays – instead they buy terrible things in supermarkets tasting of soda and studded with soggy fruits. Scones take but a moment, so do try them. The savory ones are perfect to eat with cocktails and you can make them in miniature.

MAKES ABOUT 12

1⅔ cups self-rising flour

a small pinch of salt

4 tablespoons butter

⅔ cup milk, fresh or sour, or buttermilk

Mix the flour and salt in a large bowl. Rub in the butter with your fingertips until it all resembles crumbs. Mix in the milk. Form into a soft dough with a metal spatula. Knead lightly on a floured board, then pat out into a round ¾ inch thick. Cut into 2-inch rounds with a cutter or a little cup.

Place on a greased and floured baking sheet and brush with milk. Bake in a preheated oven at 425°F for 10 minutes until well risen and brown. Cool on a rack, but eat when still warm, with lots of butter, clotted cream, and jam. Yummo.

VARIATIONS

Sweet scones: Add ¼ cup sugar to the dry ingredients.

Fruit scones: Add ⅓ cup dried fruit and 2 tablespoons sugar.

Savory scones: Add ¾ cup grated hard cheese and 1 teaspoon dry mustard, or ⅓ cup minced olives, anchovies, or what you fancy.

JP

Illustrated on previous page

Naxian Cheese Coins

This is a very good receipt I got from a cousin who lives in Naxos. They are the Naxian equivalent of cheese straws and are made with a local cheese called *kefalo tiri*. Maybe you could get it at a Greek food shop, but I do not have one so I use Parmesan instead. The main thing is that it should be a very hard cheese, so perhaps any old bits of Cheddar would do as long as it is grated very finely.

½ cup (1 stick) butter, or margarine if preferred

¾ cup flour

a large pinch of salt

½ teaspoon each paprika, celery salt, and dry mustard

a large pinch of cayenne

1 cup finely grated Parmesan cheese

1 egg yolk

Keep the butter or margarine in the freezer at the ready. Sift the flour, salt, and all the dry spices into a bowl. Add the cheese. Grate the frozen butter on the coarsest side of your grater and mix into the flour with a knife or fingertips until crumb-like. Beat the egg yolk and combine with the mixture to bind it. Knead everything together until pliable. Divide into three pieces. Roll each piece in the palms of your hands to form a sausage with the diameter of a large coin. Place the sausage shapes on a board and refrigerate for at least 2 hours.

Slice into thinnish disks. Arrange on baking sheets and bake in a preheated oven at 375°F for 10–15 minutes, swapping the sheet positions at half time. The coins should be crisp and golden brown, and are perfectly splendid with a good cocktail.

JP

EVIL'S FOOD CAKE

Why this is called Devil's Food Cake I cannot imagine – it's far too good for the devil, who gets the best tunes already, according to Charles Wesley. Perhaps, in the words of David Garrick, it is because "Heaven sends us good meat, but the Devil sends cooks." Anyway, it is devilishly good.

½ cup (1 stick) unsalted butter

4 ounces bittersweet chocolate

⅓ cup light corn syrup

¼ cup packed brown sugar

½ teaspoon baking soda

4 tablespoons milk

1⅔ cups self-rising flour

a small pinch of salt

1 egg

FOR THE VANILLA BUTTER FROSTING:

½ cup (1 stick) unsalted butter

2 cups confectioners' sugar

6 drops of pure vanilla extract
(not flavoring)

FOR THE BOILED FROSTING:

1 cup + 2 tablespoons sugar

¼ cup water

1 egg white

1 ounce bittersweet chocolate

Grease and line (with parchment) 2 layer cake pans that are 8 inches across.

In a saucepan melt the butter, chocolate, syrup, and sugar, stirring regularly (do not boil). Cool. Dissolve the baking soda in 1 tablespoon of milk. Sift the flour and the salt into a bowl and make a well in the center. Beat in the chocolate mixture, the remaining milk, and the egg, using a wooden spoon, then mix in the dissolved baking soda. Place in the prepared pans, dividing equally. Bake in a preheated oven at 325°F for 35 minutes, then unmold from the pans to cool on racks.

To make vanilla butter frosting, blend all the ingredients in a food processor until soft and creamy, or beat together by hand with a wooden spoon. If you prefer, use coffee extract or rum to taste instead of the vanilla. Spread the frosting over one cake layer, then set the other layer on top.

For the top of the cake make a boiled frosting: Put the sugar and water into a heavy pan and heat gently until the sugar dissolves. Bring to a boil and continue boiling until the syrup reaches 240°F. If you don't have a candy thermometer, drop a drop of the syrup into cold water. If it makes a soft ball it is ready. Whisk the egg white to form soft peaks. Pour the syrup gradually onto it, whisking all the time, until the frosting thickens and has a rough, granular feel. Pour the frosting over the cake and smooth in whirls with a wet, warm, stainless steel knife. Sprinkle with grated chocolate just before the frosting sets.

JP

AQUITAINIAN WALNUT TORTE

One of the most remarkable women ever to be Queen of England was Eleanor of Aquitaine. Born in 1122, she divorced the King of France to marry Henry II, and founded the first home for battered wives, at Fontreveault Abbey in France. She started the idea of Romantic love and is believed to have introduced the black walnut to England, so I always think of this as her cake. The recipe, however, I owe once again to Greta Anna.

4 eggs, separated

1 cup sugar

1 pound shelled walnuts, ground to fine crumbs (about 5½ cups)

1 teaspoon baking powder

FOR THE FROSTING:

1 pound (4 cups) confectioners' sugar, sifted

6 tablespoons unsalted butter, softened

4 teaspoons finely ground coffee beans softened with a little boiling water

Beat the egg yolks and sugar lightly together until blended. Whisk the egg whites until stiff. Fold into the yolks and sugar, then gently mix in the walnut crumbs and baking powder. Pour into a buttered 8-inch round cake pan. Bake in a preheated oven at 325°F for 50–55 minutes (test with a skewer). Cool in the pan.

For the frosting, gradually beat the confectioners' sugar into the butter and flavor with the coffee. Apply to the cooled cake.

CDW

THE VILLAGE FÊTE

(*clockwise from bottom left*) Shopping at Uppingham
market for ingredients (and hats); tea in the garden with
Mrs. Edmonson and the ladies of the Women's Institute;
Clarissa makes cakes for the cake stall; hitching a ride
from the Kirby and West milkman; relaxing on Hallaton
village green at the end of the day

$\mathscr{F}$RUIT AND VEGETABLES

CLARISSA WRITES: It is a joy what a difference fresh vegetables make. Charlie Cowan, master gardener of Inveresk, tells me that except during his time in the army he has never eaten shop-bought vegetables. Oh, how I envy him. Those terrible vegetables, all characterless, pristine, and tasteless, that the supermarkets foist on us barely deserve the name. I believe the Americans have now bred a cabbage that doesn't taste of cabbage – I expect it tastes of nothing, so what's the point? Last summer I stayed with that doyenne of food tastes, Lynda Brown, and we went madly round her garden plucking whatever came to hand and flinging it on the grill. It was an exhilarating experience.

Jennifer is adamant that, with the exception of potatoes and a few root crops, vegetables should never touch water – or at most only the water that adheres after they have been rinsed and well shaken. Nothing, she declares firmly, beats a young fava bean. I actually prefer a purée of their pods. We both love bitter greens, especially Belgian endive, but beg to differ on the carrot. It is my one aversion in the food world and that is for psychological reasons!

If you can grow your own, do, or schmooze a friend who does. If this isn't possible, go to a good greengrocer or farmer's market Don't be suckered by the prettiness myth. In the vegetable, true beauty is only skin deep.

Strangely, neither Jennifer nor I are mad about fruit. I wonder if that is due to the fact that both our backgrounds have strong Far Eastern influences (in such climates, fruit has to be eaten with circumspection).

Jennifer observes Lent with enthusiasm and says that most of her fruit eating is done as a duty during her Lenten fast. She does, however, like a properly ripe pineapple, which she says are to be found in her local Warwick Way market. She likes the taste of oranges, but not the labor of preparing them, with which I agree – when I was at school I asked friends to peel oranges for me. We both love raspberries, and Jennifer particularly likes them with red currants, as she thinks the contrast so good. I like raspberries with clotted cream and yet more clotted cream.

This last year I have made a point of only eating home-grown fruit in season – I really hate tasteless supermarket fruit and fruit that has been artificially ripened. Since moving to Scotland, and having access to fruit trees again, I have found myself much fonder of fruit. One that I have rediscovered, thanks to my friend Maggie Byrne, is the medlar. This tree is rare now, which is unfortunate because when baked in the oven with a little brown sugar the fruit is a taste for the gods. Another rare fruit is the mulberry. When I was a child we had a 400-year-old tree in the garden, and our cook's mulberry ice cream was a great delight.

Recently I was in the West Indies again, and I realised I had forgotten the true taste of a banana. Sadly, all these foreign exotics don't really travel.

That's no way to handle fruit: Jennifer upsets the oranges

PARSNIP AND GARLIC PURÉE

I invented this concoction and have won over the most ardent of parsnip haters (always due to filthy boiled parsnips at school).

2 pounds parsnips

5 garlic cloves

4 tablespoons butter

⅔ cup heavy cream

salt and freshly ground pepper

Peel the parsnips, quarter them, and cut into chunks. Have ready a saucepan of boiling salted water. Throw in the garlic cloves for a few moments' boiling, retrieve with a slotted spoon, and peel. Put the parsnips and garlic in the water to boil until tender, about 5–7 minutes. Drain well and either process or put through a vegetable mill. Beat in the butter and then the cream. Season with salt and freshly ground pepper.

Place the mixture in a gratin dish, spreading it out evenly, then broil until you have a nice brown crust. You can prepare the whole thing ahead if you like and just heat it up in the oven when required. It is fantastically good and goes especially well with game or strong-flavored dishes.

JP

*B*UBBLE AND SQUEAK

I once lived with a man who could be stopped in midsentence of even the most savage argument if I started making this dish. You may imagine I am something of an expert at it.

There are three things to remember:

1. There is no substitute for lard or beef drippings – if you object, eat something else.

2. You need a really heavy frying pan.

3. The potatoes must be cold before you start.

3 cups chopped cold cooked potatoes

¼ cup drippings or lard

1 onion, minced

1½ cups chopped cooked cabbage or Brussels sprouts

salt and freshly ground pepper

Finely chop the potatoes and crush slightly. In a frying pan, melt half of the fat and lightly fry the onion. Mix in the potato and greens and season well with salt and pepper. Add more drippings or lard. Press the bubble into the hot fat and fry over a moderate heat until browned underneath – about 15 minutes. Turn the bubble over, add the last of the drippings or lard, and fry until the other side is browned.

CDW

Illustrated overleaf

$\mathcal{S}$TUFFED ARTICHOKES

We don't make enough of artichokes in Britain. I was once paid to go and teach etiquette to Yuppies, and one of the items on the agenda was the correct way to eat artichokes! Come back Queen Victoria! Eat them as you feel inspired and use your fingers.

6 large globe artichokes

1½ cups fresh bread crumbs

1 onion, minced

1 cup coarsely grated Parmesan cheese

¼ cup chopped parsley

2 garlic cloves, minced

2 tomatoes, peeled, seeded and chopped

1 tablespoon capers, cut in half

⅓ cup chopped black olives

salt and freshly ground pepper

olive oil

⅔ cup white wine

Remove the large outside leaves from the artichokes. Cut 1 inch off the top of the remaining leaves and scoop out the choke from the center of each artichoke.

Make a stuffing by mixing together the remaining ingredients, except the oil and wine, and fill the center of the artichokes. Cover the bottom of a Dutch oven, large enough to hold the artichokes comfortably, with olive oil. Heat until it is warm, then add the artichokes. Pour the white wine over, cover, and simmer gently for about 1 hour.

CDW

*P*OOR MAN'S CAVIAR

Serve this as a first course with hot brown toast and a few slices of thinly cut tomato. Caviar it ain't, but it is extremely delicious, and of course a lot cheaper.

2 large eggplants

2 tablespoons lemon juice

¼ cup olive oil

salt and freshly ground pepper

paprika

1 large onion, minced or grated

When buying eggplants make sure they are firm, unbruised, and shiny. Put them on a baking sheet and cook in a preheated oven at 425°F until they are really soft, about 45 minutes. Pierce with a skewer to make sure. When cool enough to handle, peel them. Mash the flesh in a bowl or food processor until you have produced a totally smooth paste. Mix in the lemon juice and the olive oil. Season to taste with salt, pepper, and about ½ teaspoon paprika, depending on whether you are using the hot or the sweet variety. Combine thoroughly with the onion. Place in a nice earthenware bowl, cover with plastic wrap (to avoid stinking out the refrigerator with onion), and chill until very cold.

JP

*E*ASY ONION SOUP WITH STILTON

This is a very quick and easy onion soup, and a great way to use up leftover wine or beer and post-Christmas Stilton or even Stilton rind. I tend to make this recipe using half wine or beer and half stock, but you can just as easily use all stock and add a glass of wine or beer at the end of cooking. If you don't have any homemade stock, use canned.

2 medium onions per person, chopped

2 tablespoons butter or 1 tablespoon olive oil per person

salt and freshly ground pepper

1¼ cups liquid (see above) per person

a pinch of fresh thyme or winter savory

Stilton cheese

In a heavy saucepan, heat the fat and sauté the onions. The color of the finished soup depends on how much you caramelize the onions. I don't like dark brown onion soup, so I cook them to a light gold. It is entirely a matter of personal preference. Season with salt and pepper.

Add the liquid and bring to a boil. Adjust the seasoning and add the thyme. Cover and simmer fiercely for 30–40 minutes.

If you are using Stilton rind, grate it finely. Otherwise, chop the cheese. In either case, add it halfway through the cooking and stir well. If adding wine or beer to stock, do so 10 minutes before the end.

Serve with croutons.

CDW

REEN FISH SOUP

This recipe was created by Marion James of the Croque-en-Bouche restaurant in Malvern Wells. I am not the first to reproduce it, and indeed I came across it in Lindsay Bareham's wonderful *A Celebration of Soup*. However, I spoke to Marion and she tells me that she has now changed the recipe, to add lemon grass and ginger. I have not tried this and have difficulty in changing the original, as I like it so much.

¾ pound broccoli rabe (rapini) or ordinary broccoli

2 tablespoons butter

1 onion, thinly sliced

1 young leek, thinly sliced

salt and freshly ground pepper

3 tablespoons flour

1 quart fish stock flavored with nutmeg and fennel

1 pound assorted white fish fillet, skinned and cut in large pieces

⅔ cup heavy cream

Peel the broccoli stems, then chop all the broccoli. Cook in a little lightly salted water until tender. Drain, reserving the cooking water.

Melt the butter in a heavy saucepan and soften the onion and the leek, but do not brown. Season with salt and pepper. Add the flour and stir gently for a few minutes. Add a little stock, still stirring. Continue to add all but ⅔ cup of the stock. Simmer for 10 minutes.

Check the seasoning, and add the fish. Cook for 1 minute, then set aside to cool slightly.

Transfer to a blender, add the cooked broccoli, and process till smooth. Return to the pan, add the cream, and reheat gently. The reserved stock and broccoli water can be used to thin the soup, if desired.

CDW

*B*EANZ MEANZ FITZ

I have a great friend who used to live in Cockermouth, Cumberland, in a large country house called "The Fitz" where I learned this receipt, hence the name.

olive oil

lemon juice

salt and freshly ground
black pepper

6 slices of bacon, cut into
little strips

1½ pounds shelled, fresh, young
fava beans (about 4 cups)

4 hard-cooked eggs, peeled and
left in cold water

parsley and chives

1½ 2oz-cans anchovy fillets

Make a dressing with about ⅔ cup of best olive oil, adding lemon juice and seasoning to taste; keep it quite tart. For easy mixing, make it in a jar. Broil or fry the bacon until quite crisp and drain on paper towels. Put the beans into boiling salted water and cook until just tender; drain and "refresh" under cold running water, then peel. Pat the eggs dry (keeping them in water helps to avoid that dark line around the yolk) and chop roughly together with a good amount of parsley and snipped chives.

Lay the beans in some ravishing china dish, sprinkle with the bacon pieces, pile the eggs and herbs on next, and lattice the top with the anchovy fillets. Chill slightly. Just before serving, give the dressing a good shake and drizzle all over the beans. Bring to the table with some good crusty bread and unsalted butter. I think young fava beans picked straight from the garden are the most superior vegetable of all.

JP

RATIN OF BEETS

When I am asked, what is the one book everyone should own, the late Jane Grigson's *Vegetable Book* is high on the list, and this recipe comes from it. I love beets – all that wonderful medieval vulgarity. If you have a microwave, cook them in it and then peel them – it saves so much mess.

6 beets, boiled and peeled

¾ cup grated Cheddar cheese

½ cup grated Parmesan cheese

1½–2 cups heavy cream

salt and freshly ground pepper

bread crumbs

butter

Chop the beets coarsely. Butter a gratin dish and sprinkle a third of the mixed cheeses over the bottom. Put in half the beets and another third of the cheese, then repeat. Pour in enough cream to come to the top of the beets. Season with salt and pepper. Scatter with a few bread crumbs and dot with a little butter. Bake in a preheated oven at 350°F for 15 minutes.

CDW

*P*UMPKIN-PROSCIUTTO GNOCCHI

I think this dish comes from Mantua, where the pumpkin is the emblem of the city and where the best *"zucche gialle"* are grown.

1 small sugar pumpkin

1 egg, lightly beaten

freshly grated Parmesan (¼ cup for cooking)

6 ounces prosciutto or any smoked ham, minced

1¼ cups flour

salt and freshly ground pepper

a good scraping of freshly grated nutmeg

To cook the pumpkin, cut it in half, remove the seeds and fibers, and place it cut-side down in a buttered baking dish. Bake in a low oven for about an hour until very tender. Scoop out the flesh into a large bowl, then mash it or purée in a food processor (if necessary, press through a strainer to remove fibers). Measure 1 cup into a mixing bowl.

Whisk in the egg followed by the ¼ cup of cheese and the ham. Stir in the flour little by little with a wooden spoon, then beat away for 4 minutes or so until the mixture is rather elastic. Add salt, pepper, and nutmeg to taste. Beat again for another minute.

Have a large saucepan of boiling water ready. Make little oval shapes of the dough, using 2 teaspoons if it helps. Drop the gnocchi, a few at a time, into the water. When they rise to the surface, remove carefully with a slotted spoon to drain on paper towels, then transfer them with care to a fine buttered baking dish. Continue this poaching until all the dough is used up.

When you wish to eat, reheat the gnocchi in the oven at 350°F for 15 minutes. Serve with a bowl of Parmesan to scatter at personal whim.

JP

$\mathcal{P}$ARSNIPS ROASTED WITH MACE AND BRANDY

This is from Michelle Beridale Johnson's good little British Museum cookbook.
It is an unusual way of serving parsnips, which works very well.

6 parsnips, trimmed but not peeled

2 tablespoons butter

½ wineglass(2-2½fl oz) of brandy

1 teaspoon ground mace

Boil the parsnips for 15 minutes. Cool slightly, then peel and slice. Heat the butter, brandy, and mace in a pan, put in the parsnips, and heat through. Reduce the liquid to a glaze and serve hot.

CDW

 TOMATO SUMMER PUDDING

I thought this up while daydreaming over that splendid Italian peasant dish, *Panzanella*. It is essential that you find really good, sweet tomatoes – none of those tasteless numbers. *Passata* is a purée of tomatoes, sold in Italian food shops; or you can use good canned tomato purée.

fresh plum or vine-ripened tomatoes – they must have a good taste

salt and freshly ground black pepper

sugar

tomato passata

lemon juice

Worcestershire and hot pepper sauce

stale Italian bread, de-crusted and sliced

minced garlic

virgin olive oil

a large bunch of fresh basil

Have enough tomatoes to overfill the mold you will use. Dip into boiling water and peel them. Chop roughly and sprinkle with good sea salt and black pepper plus a tiny bit of sugar. Pour some *passata* into a large soup plate and season with lemon juice and Worcestershire sauce, and maybe a touch of hot pepper sauce. Soak the bread slices briefly in this mixture and line your mold with them, leaving no cracks nor crannies.

To the tomatoes add as much minced garlic as you fancy, plus a good measure of olive oil and lots of torn-up basil leaves. Adjust the seasoning and pour the whole lot into the bread-lined mold. Seal the top with more soaked bread. Place a receptacle on top with weights (such as cans of food) and leave overnight in the refrigerator. Unmold onto a fine dish and surround with goodies – quail eggs, olives, sweet peppers, capers, or what you will. A bowl of sour cream might be handed around with it, or good homemade mayonnaise.

JP

Illustrated overleaf

 Guacamole

This famous Mexican avocado mash can be served as a first course with some brown toast, but is usually used as a dip – not a form of eating I particularly favor, but if you do, serve with corn or tortilla chips. Be warned: a hot chili pepper's fire is contained in its seeds and pale interior spines. To temper the chili's pungency, remove both with a sharp knife, but do not touch your face or eyes until you have washed your hands or you will be in agony.

2 tablespoons minced or grated mild onion

1 small hot green chili pepper, seeded and minced

4 sprigs of fresh cilantro leaves, minced

¼ teaspoon salt

2 good-sized avocados

1 large tomato, seeded and chopped

2 tablespoons minced red onion

1 tablespoon lime or lemon juice

Mix the mild onion, chili, half the cilantro, and the salt in a mortar. Pound into a paste. Scoop the avocado flesh into a bowl. Mash the flesh well, then add the paste from the mortar. Mix thoroughly, and stir in the tomato, red onion, and the rest of the cilantro. Sprinkle the surface with the lime or lemon juice. Cover tightly with plastic wrap and chill until wanted. Just before serving, give it a good stir and adjust seasoning.

JP

*L*AVER AND POTATO CAKES

I am always buying cans of laver "bread" – which is really a mush of seaweed – because I love it fried with bacon. One day in an effort to impress my friend Marianne, who makes lemon curd rather than throw away an egg yolk, and creates sumptuous dishes out of nothing, I decided to do something else with it. Laver bread is, of course, native to Wales, so more Brownie points and less hanging off cliffs for me!

a bunch of scallions, minced

2 cups mashed potato

1 can laver bread

salt and freshly ground pepper

1 egg

butter and oil

Mix the scallions with the potatoes and laver bread and season well with salt and pepper. Bind with the egg. Mold into small cakes.

In a heavy frying pan, heat butter and oil together. You need to fry these cakes at quite a high temperature or they will fall apart. Fry until browned on both sides, then drain on paper towels and serve.

CDW

ELON STUFFED WITH RASPBERRIES

I took this confection to Glyndebourne as my contribution to a splendid picnic before the opera.

1 pound raspberries

sugar

Grand Marnier or Cointreau

1 medium-sized ripe Ogen or cantaloupe melon

Strew the raspberries with enough sugar to suit your taste. Pour a small glass of the liqueur over them and leave for a few hours to infuse.

Cut a slice off the top end of the melon of your choice (this will be the lid, so make it a fairly thick slice). Scoop out the flesh and discard the seeds. Chop the flesh and add to the raspberries. Put this mixture back into the melon skin. Replace the lid and secure with tape. Put it into a plastic bag and secure the opening. Chill well before serving.

JP

Mashed Potato and Yogurt

I was reluctant to try this as it smacked of ruining things for the sake of calories, but then I remembered that the Indians often eat yogurt with potato, and they are, or have been until recently, free of the dieting vice.

2 pounds potatoes

4 tablespoons butter

¼ cup plain yogurt

salt and freshly ground pepper

chopped fresh mint

Boil the potatoes in their skins. When they are cool enough to handle, peel them. Mash with the butter and mix in the yogurt. Season with salt and pepper and sprinkle with chopped mint.

CDW

Jennifer and Clarissa on microwaves

CLARISSA: The trouble with microwaves is that they never smell of anything. All you get is mnmnmnmnm … ping.

JENNIFER: I've never used a microwave. They frighten me. I've heard terrible tales about coffee boiling over or the spoon doing something peculiar.

CLARISSA: Well, they're not too bad for fish or scrambled eggs.

JENNIFER: How come?

CLARISSA: Well, if you are doing scrambled eggs for loads of people, you don't have to keep stirring them all the time. You put them in for one and a half minutes, whisk them, and then put them back for another minute and a half. You actually get quite palatable scrambled eggs – not as good as the real thing of course, but not bad.

PEACHES CARDINAL HUME

This is one of the best ways of eating peaches. An old receipt, I have added Hume to the original Cardinale because the saintly man lives around the corner from me. I often have chats with him from my motorbike and I love him.

3¼ cups sugar

6 cups water

1 vanilla bean

10 ripe large peaches

1 pound raspberries

Put 2¼ cups of the sugar into a saucepan large enough to hold the peaches. Add the water and the vanilla bean and bring to a boil, gently to begin with, stirring until the sugar dissolves. When simmering put in the peaches. Bring back to simmering point and very gently poach for 8 minutes. Remove the peaches and peel while still warm. The syrup can be bottled and used to poach other fruits. Put the peaches into a beautiful glass dish and chill.

Purée the raspberries with the remaining sugar and strain through a sieve if you wish to get rid of the seeds. When ready to eat, pour the glorious red purée over the succulent peaches. Decorate with mint leaves dragged through confectioners' sugar.

JP

 GREEN BANANA CLATCH

This is a dish we all invented while in Barbados. My friend Moira Elias, who comes from the Scottish Borders, named it a "clatch," which means a mudpie in dialect. I am rather proud of this dish because it started as a rescue exercise.

The dish should be made with small green bananas, known as figs in Barbados, but you cannot buy these here, so buy green (unripe) bananas. If you cannot find tamarind chutney, you can use block tamarind pulp. This should be softened in water and then fried up with the other vegetables.

10 green bananas

4 onions, chopped

6 tomatoes, peeled, seeded and chopped

3 garlic cloves, minced

2 hot chili peppers, minced, or a dash of hot pepper sauce

oil

salt and freshly ground pepper

2 tablespoons tamarind chutney

In a pressure cooker, boil the bananas, in their skins, for 20 minutes. Without a pressure cooker they will take about 40 minutes cooking as they need to fall apart when peeled.

Sauté the onions, tomatoes, garlic, and chilies in a little oil. Season generously with salt and pepper. Mash the bananas well, then vigorously stir in the fried vegetables and tamarind chutney. Serve hot.

CDW

$\mathcal{C}$ HERRIES JUBILEE

Bulgaria produces some first-rate canned cherries, if you can find them, or, if they are in season, you can use fresh ones stewed in syrup. Ice cream is served with these cherries, so buy or make the best vanilla you can.

a 1-pound can pitted black cherries

grated zest of 1 lemon

½ cup sugar

a large pinch of ground cinnamon

3 tablespoons kirsch or similar liqueur

2 teaspoons cornstarch

½ cup Cognac

vanilla ice cream

Drain the cherries, but reserve the juice. Mix the fruit with the lemon zest, half of the sugar, the cinnamon, and liqueur and leave to steep until needed, at least 2 hours – the longer the better.

When you are about to eat this dessert, blend the cornstarch with the steeping juices from the cherries until quite smooth. Add a few spoons of the canned juice. Pour into a frying pan and stir over a low heat until clear and thickened. Pour in more canned cherry juice, if necessary. Stir in the cherries to heat through. Sprinkle with the remaining sugar, add the Cognac, and then set fire to the whole mixture, spooning the juices over and over until the flames abate. Serve poured over the ice cream. Very luscious.

JP

PEASE PUDDING

"Pease pudding hot, pease pudding cold,
Pease pudding in the pot nine days old."

Thus went the old skipping rhyme. I love pease pudding with ham or indeed any old thing. It is as old as our history and was sold by street vendors well into the nineteenth century. You can now buy ham bouillon cubes, which will do if you are not boiling a ham. In Scotland, they sell smoked pork ribs in the supermarket and ham hocks are easy to come by.

2½ pounds (5½ cups) split peas, soaked overnight

6 cups of ham stock or 6 cups of water and 2 ham hocks

2 tablespoons butter

2 egg yolks

salt and freshly ground pepper

Tie the peas loosely in a cloth and boil in the ham stock (or in the pan with your water and ham hocks) for 1½ hours.

Remove from the pan and rub the peas through a strainer. Dry over a gentle heat till thick. Stir in the butter and egg yolks, and season well with salt and pepper.

CDW

ou cou

Cou cou is native to Barbados. It is a dish traditionally served with flying fish and is an interesting combination of okra and cornmeal. I had always had trouble with my okra going slimy, but I have now been taught that if you peel the stem end to a point, much as you would sharpen a pencil, this will not happen.

12 young okras

3 cups boiling water

1 small hot chili pepper, seeded and minced

salt

2 cups yellow cornmeal

3 cups cold water

2 tablespoons butter

Slice the okra diagonally into ¼-inch rings and put in a heavy pan. Add the 3 cups of boiling water, the chili, and salt to taste and cook for 10 minutes.

Sift the cornmeal into a bowl and mix well with the 3 cups of cold water. Off the heat, mix the cornmeal into the okra and its cooking liquid. Return to a medium heat and stir frequently until the mixture is smooth and thick. Turn into a serving dish and dot with the butter. Serve hot.

CDW

LAMICHE

Both the word and often the actuality of quiche make my flesh crawl. I left school in 1964, just as England discovered the quiche. Quite good cooks were ruined overnight. It was as damaging to the food culture of the British Isles as the hamburger. I spent my adolescence avoiding it, and nothing since has changed my mind. Flamiche is the Flemish answer to the quiche. People forget that Flanders was once a major world power; that William the Conqueror's marriage to Matilda of Flanders was on a par with Queen Victoria marrying her plumber; that the Flemish weavers held the wool trade to ransom. Flamiche is made with brioche dough and can be filled with whatever you like. I have given a leek filling – for Wales, you understand.

MAKES 2

FOR THE BRIOCHE DOUGH:

a 0.6-ounce cake fresh compressed yeast or 1 package active dry yeast

¼ cup lukewarm water

4 cups white bread flour

6 extra large eggs

1½ teaspoons salt

2 tablespoons superfine sugar

1 cup (2 sticks) unsalted butter, softened

Put the yeast and water into a small bowl and leave until dissolved. Sift the flour into a large bowl, break the eggs into it, and add the salt, sugar, and yeast mixture. Blend with the fingertips to make a dough. If the dough is sticky, add more flour.

On a floured surface, knead the dough for 5 minutes until it is smooth and very elastic. Add the softened butter and knead into the dough. Form into a ball. Transfer to a lightly oiled bowl, turn the dough so that it is coated with oil, and cover with a damp cloth. Leave to rise for about 2 hours until it has doubled in size. Then chill the dough for at least 4 hours.

For the filling, melt the butter in a frying pan, add the leeks, and season with salt and pepper. Cover and cook over a low heat for 20 minutes until the leeks are soft.

FOR THE LEEK FILLING:

2 tablespoons butter

**1½ pounds leeks, sliced
lengthwise and quartered**

salt and freshly ground pepper

2 egg yolks

⅓ cup heavy cream

Butter two 10-inch round cake pans. Punch down the dough and divide in half. Roll out each portion to a 14-inch round and use to line the pans, letting surplus dough hang over the side. Spread the leeks over the dough. Beat the egg yolks with the cream, season, and pour over the leeks. Lift up the overhanging dough to cover half the filling. Leave for 15 minutes.

Bake in a preheated oven at 400°F for 45 minutes until the crust is brown and the filling set.

CDW

ESCADO COCHO

This is a recipe from Tangier, once known as Carthage. If Hannibal had defeated Scipio Africanus, its citizens might have ruled the world. Do not be alarmed by the amount of garlic in this recipe. Uncut garlic has a gentle, milky flavor and texture when cooked. Just be careful not to cut the cloves until they are cooked and you will be agreeably surprised.

2 tablespoons olive oil

½ green bell pepper, diced

1 large ripe tomato, chopped

1 dried hot red chili pepper, crumbled

6–8 garlic cloves, unpeeled

salt

1½ cups fresh lima beans

¼ cup water

a 1½-pound fillet of white fish (hake, halibut, cod, or haddock), cut into 6 pieces

Heat the oil in a Dutch oven and gently fry the green pepper, tomato, chili, and garlic cloves, taking care that the garlic cloves remain whole. Add a little salt and cook for about 5 minutes. Add the beans and the water. Cover and cook for 20 minutes.

Place the fish in the sauce, making sure it is immersed in the liquid, and cook for a further 10–15 minutes, uncovered, until the fish is cooked. Check the seasoning.

Serve with couscous and salad.

CDW

Whatever the weather, the show must go on. Clarissa and Jennifer survived the rain and the cold in their own inimitable style

$\mathcal{G}$AME

CLARISSA WRITES: People have these old-fashioned, pre-conceived notions about game in Great Britain. They seem to think that it is the province of either the rich or the aristocracy, or else that it is putrid and maggot-ridden. All this is nonsense.

You can now buy game in the supermarket here, and this has the advantage of being prepared in amorphous little packages bearing little resemblance to the original creature. However, as Jennifer – who will shop in such places – points out, it is very seldom properly hung. While very few people nowadays want to hang game until the head falls off, it is necessary to let it hang for a few days to a week in order to enhance the flavor and to tenderize it in the same way as meat. Another disadvantage of supermarket game is that it is not particularly cheap.

However, game can be extremely cheap if bought from the right sources. The average price of a dressed (i.e. plucked) pheasant varies from £2.50 to £4, and if you live in shooting areas it can be as little as £1.50. If you compare this with the price of a free-range chicken you can see that it is ridiculously underpriced and even measures up well to a battery fowl. In the USA, you may have to order game birds directly from a game farm, but some specialty food stores also stock a good selection.

Farmed venison has the advantage of being consistently tender and young, but to my mind it does not have the flavor of the wild. Still, farmed venison is easier to cook, and you have to be careful when choosing wild meat – it is essential to use a good butcher.

Deer kidneys are totally delicious. They are hard to find and by law come from farmed beasts. Venison liver is also good, but is disastrous if overcooked.

Wild duck is surprisingly cheap and has more meat than you would expect. It is a total mystery to me why we don't simply deal with the urban plagues of Canada geese by eating them, preferably stuffed with olives and prunes.

Pigeons, which are vermin, are not eaten nearly enough. And as for rabbit…Jennifer makes the point that people have been turned against rabbit because they ate it badly cooked as children or because of the horror of myxomatosis. It is time to set aside these prejudices. Rabbit is cheap, plentiful, and delicious. If more were eaten the price would drop further. At the moment tons are shot and left to lie, as keepers don't find a big enough market to make them worth collecting. Grouse and partridge are luxury items, but still worth buying as a treat.

Once upon a time, I cooked and worked on a pheasant farm in Sussex, and had plenty of opportunity to cook all types of game. I assure you that with a little concentration it is easy to cook.

I don't personally have much truck with the cholesterol myth. I eat a great deal of animal fat while having the cholesterol level of a two year old. However, it is true that game has no fat (a fact that has to be overcome when cooking, either by larding or marinating). It is, therefore, something of a mystery to me why it is not more widely eaten. I don't know where this series will take us, but the upper echelons of the Scottish aristocracy are our aim, and the Scots are a nation brave enough to bear our eccentricities.

When Jennifer Last Shot

JENNIFER: The last time I shot was a million years ago. I was shooting chukhar in Bengazi with the Lancers and a very volatile Italian consul who shot everybody in sight.

CLARISSA: Forgive my ignorance, but what is chukhar?

JENNIFER: A delicious bird – a bit like a big partridge. I used to roast it in a Baby Belling and serve it with bread sauce. I adore bread sauce.

PARTRIDGES WITH CABBAGE

Almost above all other game birds, I love partridges. I like watching them alive, and I love to eat them "plump as bishops," as Browning says. Ian MacCall, of the Scottish Game Conservancy, tells me partridges are on the increase due to the simple expedient of leaving the borders of fields unsprayed. When you tell people you are going to cook this dish they look askance, as if the cabbage will spoil the birds, but I find it excellent and a good way of dealing with older birds.

1 medium head cabbage (I prefer savoy), shredded

4 tablespoons butter, lard, or bacon drippings

1 partridge per person

salt and freshly ground pepper

¼ teaspoon paprika

juniper berries

1¼ cups heavy cream

Parboil the shredded cabbage in salted water for 10 minutes. Drain well.

In a heavy pan, melt the fat and brown the partridges on all sides. Add the cabbage, season with salt and pepper, and add the paprika and a few juniper berries. Cover and cook for 20 minutes.

Add the cream, mix well, and adjust the seasoning. Cover and cook for a further 10 minutes.

CDW

Clarissa's tip

It's better not to buy your game from the supermarket, as you can't tell how old it is. Once a bird has been plucked and skinned, it's impossible to tell its age.

PARTRIDGE ROASTED IN GRAPE LEAVES

Grape leaves have the ability to impart their own special flavor to the food they enwrap. Elizabeth David has a fascinating receipt for cooking the commonest of mushrooms in a grape-leaf-lined pot, which makes them taste like the most sophisticated of fungi from the forest. They do no less for these lovely little birds.

Grape leaves can now be bought in packets if you don't have a grapevine, and I find the best fat for birds is *lardo* from Italian food shops.

4 plump young partridges with their livers

salt and freshly ground pepper

4 slices of pork fatback or unsmoked bacon to cover the breasts

8 grape leaves

1 cup (2 sticks) butter

Season the birds inside and out and place the slices of fat on their little bosoms. Wrap each in a grape leaf and secure with fine string. Melt half the butter in a Dutch oven that will hold the birds comfortably. Cook the birds at a medium heat on top of the stove until the grape leaves take color, about 3–4 minutes on each side. The butter should froth a bit and achieve a hazelnut color. Each time you turn the birds, season with a little more salt and pepper and add a pat of butter until it is mostly used up. After 15 minutes, remove from the heat and let the little creatures rest on their backs for a further 15 minutes.

Remove string and grape leaves. Heat the pan again and brown the breasts very lightly, turning gently. The legs should be a nice pink when pierced. Serve on croutons with Belgian endive salad, scattered with the fried partridge livers if you managed to get them.

JP

Illustrated overleaf

$\mathscr{P}$HEASANT NORMANDY

This is a sumptuous way of preparing pheasant. It also makes the birds go quite a long way
due to the richness of the sauce and the fact that the dish arrives fully prepared at table so there is no waste
from badly carved carcasses.

4 sweet, firm apples

½ cup (1 stick) butter

1 teaspoon brown sugar

2 young pheasants (called a brace if one is a hen and the other a cock)

⅔ cup Calvados

2½ cups heavy cream

salt and freshly ground pepper

Peel and core the apples, slice into rings, and fry in 4 tablespoons of the butter. Add the sugar and cook until golden brown and slightly caramelized. Reserve.

Melt the rest of the butter in a flameproof casserole large enough to hold the birds. Brown the creatures on all sides, turning and coating with the butter. Cover with the lid and place in a preheated oven at 375°F to cook for 40 minutes; or you can cook them on top of the stove, turning at half time.

Carve the birds into good-size pieces and lay them in a shallow gratin dish. Make sure to pick every little piece of meat from the bones. Place the legs at either end. Keep warm. Scrape any morsels from the carving into the casserole juices and heat until bubbling, then pour in the warmed Calvados. Set fire to the mixture, but take care not to singe your eyelashes. Roll the juices round and round until the flames subside. Add the cream and continue cooking, stirring the while with a wooden spoon, until the sauce thickens. Season to taste.

Place the apple rings over the pheasant pieces, then pour the sauce over the whole dish and bring to table. If you prefer, you can serve the apple rings separately. Wild rice with fried celery would be excellent with this dish, and a watercress salad should suffice.

JP

*B*OILED SQUABS AND HAM

In the Middle Ages, it was customary to simmer game and meat together. I like this blending of flavors, and the fat of the ham prevents the pigeon from becoming dry. The great dovecotes of mediaeval castles were not for show: they were a meat source – a living refrigerator. Young birds were taken whenever needed for the kitchens, and pigeons were much eaten. You could use the farmed young pigeons known as squabs, but cook them for much less time.

4 pigeons or squabs

1 faggot of herbs (bouquet garni)

a 2-pound piece of picnic ham

1 onion, studded with cloves

1 celery stalk, chopped

2 carrots, chopped

freshly ground pepper

2 pounds leaf spinach

Place all the ingredients, except the spinach, in a large pan. Cover with cold water and season with pepper. Bring to a boil, skimming the surface, then cover and simmer gently for 1–1½ hours or until tender.

Wash the spinach well, then cook until wilted. Drain well.

Drain the ham and pigeons. Place the ham on a large serving dish. Surround with spinach and lay the pigeons on top. Serve hot. Parsley sauce and Cumberland sauce go well with this.

CDW

PIGEON BREAST WITH HONEY AND GINGER

The late Archie Coates was probably the world's most famous pigeon shot, and his wife Prue, author of several excellent game cookbooks, may well have cooked more pigeons than anyone else. I am indebted to her for this delicious recipe. It is equally good hot or cold. The quantities given for the sauce will make more than needed, so you can have great fun finding other uses for it.

FOR THE SAUCE:

6 tablespoons sugar

⅔ cup water

½ cup stem ginger in syrup, drained

2 tablespoons honey

8 squab breasts

4 tablespoons butter

juice of ½ lemon

salt and freshly ground pepper

For the sauce, dissolve the sugar in the water and boil for 4 minutes without stirring. In a blender pulverize the ginger, add the honey, and process, gradually pouring in the sugar syrup. Blend till smooth. This can be done in advance and kept in the refrigerator.

Heat the butter in a frying pan till foaming and cook the squab breasts for 3 minutes on each side. Add ¼ cup of the ginger sauce and cook for a minute more. Remove the squab breasts, slice them lengthwise, and fan out on warmed plates. Add the lemon juice to the pan and cook until the sauce is thick and syrupy. Season to taste. Pour the sauce over the squab breasts and serve hot. If serving cold, add thinly sliced fennel dressed with oil and lemon juice.

CDW

QUAIL

Quail are dear little mouthfuls, but as they are no longer wild they have very little flavor. However, they are very tender and good to eat when tarted up in various guises. These are excellent.

4 tablespoons unsalted butter

2 garlic cloves, minced

1 tablespoon honey

juice of 1 lemon

salt and freshly ground black pepper

4 quail

Melt the butter in a little frying pan, add the garlic, and sauté gently until softened but not browned. Add the honey and lemon juice. Stir until mixed, then season generously with salt and pepper.

Place the quail in a small roasting pan and pour the contents of the frying pan over them. Brush the insides of the birds with some of the juices. Roast in a preheated oven at 450°F for 10 minutes. Remove from the oven, baste with the juices, and finish under the broiler until they are burnished and browned. Serve with a good salad.

JP

Jennifer's tip

When sautéeing game, or indeed any other meat, make sure you brown it properly and quickly. This is really important for the flavor.

UNTREATH ROAST GROUSE

This is a perfect way of cooking the slightly older birds you buy later in the shooting season. Some people actually prefer grouse cooked this way, whatever the age.

apples

butter

1 grouse per person

salt and freshly ground pepper

sliced bacon

Place a piece of apple and a pat of butter inside each bird. Season inside and out with salt and pepper and wrap well in bacon slices. Stand in ½ inch of water in a roasting pan and cover with a lid of foil. Roast in a preheated oven at 300°F for 45 minutes.

Remove the foil lid and pour the liquid from the pan. Unwrap the bacon. Zap up the oven temperature to 450°F and roast for 10 more minutes to brown the birds.

CDW

Clarissa's tip

If you are fortunate enough to be able to choose your own game from a shoot, you can tell if it's a young bird by feeling its claws and beak.

GUINEA FOWL

I remember cooking this after Mass at the London Oratory, which was fraught with excitement after a mad woman had stalked up to the altar and emptied a bag full of rubbish on the steps, old dog food cans and milk cartons for the most part. She was yelling in some foreign tongue and had to be led away.

3 ounces salt pork or bacon, diced (about ⅓ cup)

1 cup chopped shallots

olive oil

the bird's liver or a chicken liver, chopped

⅔ cup chopped black olives

1 tablespoon fresh thyme leaves

1 guinea fowl or Cornish hen

Fry the salt pork and the shallots in about 3 tablespoons of olive oil until they are beginning to brown (if using bacon, use just 1 tablespoon oil). Add the liver and stir-fry for a minute. Add the olives and thyme and mix well together. Remove from the heat and stuff into the bird's cavity. Brush the bird all over with olive oil, place in a snug roasting pan and cook in a preheated oven at 425°F for an hour. Baste well every 20 minutes while you are having your pre-prandial cocktails.

Serve with nice little potatoes and some juicy sautéed Belgian endive, which goes very well with a bird.

JP

Jennifer's tip

You have to use lots of fat in game to lubricate it: it has little fat of its own.

DUCK WITH QUINCES

Somewhere out there is a poem, the theme of which is that God, fed up with the world he has created, creates the duck and laughs with joy. Much as I like watching ducks, I love eating them better – indeed, it will be on the menu of my last meal if and when they hang me! This is a Georgian recipe collected by that indefatigable and excellent American cookery writer, Paula Wolfert, for her book *The Cooking of the Eastern Mediterranean.*

1 wild duck

½ teaspoon black peppercorns

1 cinnamon stick

1 small onion, halved

3 large quinces

½ teaspoon ground cinnamon

sea salt

freshly ground black pepper

1 lemon, halved

3 tablespoons olive oil

2 onions, chopped

Remove any excess fat from the duck's cavity. Prick the skin all over with a fork and place the duck, breast-side up, in a Dutch oven. Add 2 cups of water, the peppercorns, cinnamon stick, and halved onion. Bring to a boil. Wet a sheet of parchment paper and cover the duck with it. Cover the pot tightly and cook over a low heat for 1 hour.

Wash, dry, peel, and core the quinces. Cut them into eighths. Mix the debris from this operation with the ground cinnamon, salt, pepper, and the pulp of half of the lemon and set aside.

Remove the duck from the pot and set aside. Skim the fat from the cooking juices, strain, and reserve. Stuff the duck with the quince debris. Rub the skin of the duck with the remaining lemon half. Set the duck on a rack in a roasting pan and roast in a preheated oven at 350°F for 1 hour until crisp and golden. Baste occasionally with salted water. Raise the oven temperature to 475°F and roast for a further 20 minutes.

Heat the olive oil in a frying pan and sauté the quinces and chopped onions until golden. Cover and cook for a further 10 minutes, then mix in the cooking juices from the duck and simmer until the quinces are tender and the sauce thickens. Adjust the seasoning. Serve the duck with the onion and quince sauce.

CDW

$\mathcal{J}$ALMI OF GAME

This nice old-fashioned dish should ideally be made with half-roasted gamebirds, starting from scratch, but I find it a useful way to use up the remains of half-eaten birds. If you go to a dinner party during the game season, you often see untutored people merely toying with their birds, leaving a wealth of good meat on the carcass. In such cases, I beg the leftovers from mine host and render them into the desired Salmi. Here I give you the authentic method.

any form of game bird, roasted very rare, to produce about 1 pound meat

4 shallots, minced, plus 1 whole shallot

a bouquet garni including a blade of mace

black peppercorns

thinly pared zest of 1 orange

salt and freshly ground pepper

4 tablespoons butter

1 heaping tablespoon flour

⅔ cup red or white wine

2 cups sliced mushrooms, sautéed in butter

lemon juice

bread for croutons

Carve the meat off the bones into slices as neatly as possible. Reserve. Remove any skin or fat, bash the carcasses, and place together in a saucepan. Leave in the hearts and livers, but remove the rather bitter, spongy substance from the insides. Cover with water or stock. Add a whole shallot, the bouquet garni, a few peppercorns, and the orange zest. Bring to a boil and simmer for about an hour. Strain, return to the saucepan, and reduce to 2 cups of stock. Season.

In another saucepan, large enough to receive all the ingredients, melt the butter and fry the minced shallots until soft and yellow. Add the flour and cook for a couple of minutes, then pour in the stock little by little, stirring away to make a sauce. Let it simmer for half an hour or more until quite thick. Add the wine and the mushrooms. Simmer for 5 minutes.

Turn the heat very low. Place the slices of meat in the sauce to heat through for 10 minutes; on no account let them boil which would ruin them. Check seasoning and add a touch of lemon juice to taste. Have ready some good white bread fried crisp in butter. Arrange the Salmi in the center of a warmed dish and surround with snippets of the bread. Serve with a salad.

JP

ƒLOE GIN DUCK

Again my thanks to Prue Coates for this recipe. In all the years of my alcoholic indulgence, I wept
as I threw away the sloes from my sloe gin. Now that I no longer make it, I have found this recipe, so I
offer it to you with affection.

2 mallard ducks

salt and freshly ground pepper

**¼ cup gin-soaked sloes from
your sloe gin making**

2 shallots, peeled

½ cup (1 stick) butter

⅔ cup stock

red wine or balsamic vinegar

Salt and pepper the ducks well and stuff with the fruit and the
shallots.

Melt the butter in a roasting pan and add the ducks. Roast in a
preheated oven at 425°F for 45 minutes, or longer if the ducks are
large or you don't like them pink. Baste frequently.

Remove the ducks to a warm place. Spoon the fat from the pan,
then add the stock and a splash of vinegar and let it bubble on top
of the stove. Meanwhile, spoon the fruit and shallots from inside
the ducks and strain, pressing through as much of the fruit as
possible. Add the resulting purée to the stock mixture. Reduce,
check the seasoning, and pour over the carved duck.

CDW

Clarissa's tip

Don't be afraid to use your hands when you're cooking. It's
becoming such an unhandling age. But as Jennifer always says, you
must eat germs in order to innoculate yourself against them. She
was brought up on water from the Yangtze, and no one in her
family has ever suffered from gippy tummy.

*E*LIZABETHAN RABBIT

A rabbit warren was part of the live larder of an Elizabethan home. Rabbits were still hard to rear and so were regarded as luxury food. It has been said that the Middle Ages ended at the Battle of Bosworth in 1485, but the Elizabethans were still close enough in culinary terms to enjoy the use of fruit in meat dishes, a practice that I believe had come back from the Crusades.

1 rabbit, cut up

flour for dusting

¼ cup lard or drippings

3 Jerusalem artichokes, sliced

2 onions, minced

2 carrots, diced

¾ cup sliced mushrooms

1¼ cups red wine

1 bouquet garni

2 apples, peeled and chopped

1 cup grapes, halved and seeded

⅓ cup raisins

grated zest and juice of ½ orange

⅔ cup chicken stock

salt and freshly ground pepper

Flour the rabbit pieces and brown them well in lard or drippings in a Dutch oven. Remove. Fry the artichokes, onions, carrots and mushrooms in the Dutch oven for a few minutes. Pour the wine over and reduce slightly. Return the rabbit pieces and add all the other ingredients. Cook in a preheated oven at 350°F for 2 hours.

A variation on this dish, which I like very much, is to stop the cooking at 1½ hours, transfer to a deep-dish pie pan, add hard-cooked eggs and globe artichoke hearts, cover with a pastry crust and bake to serve as a pie.

CDW

RABBIT WITH ANCHOVIES AND CAPERS

I have no idea how the rabbit got involved with Easter, but whatever the reason, my feeling is eat it. It can be cooked in a hundred different ways, it has hardly any fat, and the flesh is delectable. The following receipt has the surprising addition of anchovies and is very good indeed.

4 salted anchovies, or 8 anchovy fillets in oil

4 pounds rabbit pieces

6 tablespoons olive oil

2½ cups dry white wine, or 1¼ cups each dry vermouth and water

juice of ½ lemon

4 garlic cloves

1 onion, thinly sliced

1 large carrot, thinly sliced

1 celery stalk, thinly sliced

2 bayleaves

fresh rosemary and parsley

salt and freshly ground pepper

flour seasoned with salt and pepper

1 fresh hot red or green chili pepper, chopped and pounded

½ cup capers

Put the salted anchovies into a bowl of water to soak for 20 minutes, then remove the bones and leave to dry on paper towel. Marinate the rabbit pieces in a mixture of half of the olive oil, the wine, lemon juice, 2 minced cloves of garlic, the vegetables, herbs, and a seasoning of salt and black pepper. Leave for 6 hours at least or overnight.

Take the rabbit out of the marinade, pat dry with a cloth or paper towel, and toss each piece in seasoned flour. Heat the remaining oil in a good heavy frying pan. When hot, throw in the pounded chili and then brown the rabbit pieces briskly. Place the rabbit in a Dutch oven. Pour the marinade into the hot frying pan, bring rapidly to a boil, and transfer to the Dutch oven. Cook in a preheated oven at 325°F for 45 minutes to 1 hour (pierce for tenderness).

Chop up the anchovies, capers, and the remaining garlic and simmer in ⅔ cup of the liquid from the rabbit for 10 minutes. Add this to the Dutch oven for a final amalgamation. Check seasoning and serve sprinkled with a good handful of chopped parsley. Some boiled new potatoes or fresh noodles are a good accompaniment to the dish.

JP

RABBIT WITH MUSTARD

In their brilliant book, *The Complete Mustard*, Robin Weir and Ros Mann give this traditional recipe. I love it and serve it often. My mother was Australian, so I find it impossible to be sentimental about rabbit. Myxomatosis and bad cooking drove it from our daily diet with displays of the same panic that we are now exercising over beef. Wild rabbit should be soaked in milk overnight if the taste is too strong for you.

1 tablespoon olive oil

½ cup (1 stick) unsalted butter

1 rabbit, quartered

salt and freshly ground pepper

4–6 tablespoons Dijon mustard

2 shallots, minced

½ pound button mushrooms, sliced (about 3½ cups)

¼ cup brandy

1¼ cups heavy cream

1 bunch of parsley, minced

Heat the oil and butter in a large pan and lightly brown the rabbit pieces. Remove them from the pan, season with salt and pepper, and smear all over with mustard.

Sauté the shallots for 5 minutes, then stir in the mushrooms. Return the rabbit pieces to the pan, pour the brandy over, and ignite. When the flames have burned out, stir in the cream and bring to boiling point. Cover and simmer for 30 minutes until the sauce is thick and the meat tender.

Adjust seasoning and sprinkle with the parsley. Serve hot.

CDW

UGGED HARE

The hare is a curious creature, steeped in mythology and affected by the moon. It is swift-footed, and possesses fearfulness and Aphrodisian lasciviousness, qualities which are conspicuous in any self-respecting satyr; hence, it was much admired in the olden days of gods and heroes and was meant to keep you sexually attractive for nine days after consuming its flesh. Try it out for kicks – why not? My feeling is that it is one of the most delicious of meats, whether jugged, roasted, potted or what you will. If you are able to get a hare, be sure to take a receptacle with you for the blood, which is most important to this dish – the smell is filthy but the result divine. Have the hare cut up into eight pieces and proceed in the following manner.

1 young hare, or jackrabbit with its liver, heart, and blood

FOR THE MARINADE:

1 bottle of hearty red wine

⅔ cup olive oil

2 tablespoons brandy

3 onions, sliced

10 garlic cloves, crushed with a spoon

5 bayleaves, crushed

grated zest of 1 lemon

FOR THE COOKING:

heaping ½ cup flour well seasoned with salt and pepper

¾ cup diced bacon, preferably unsmoked

Marinate the hare, with its chopped liver, blood, and heart, in all the ingredients listed. Cover with plastic wrap and keep somewhere cool overnight.

Dry off the hare pieces with paper towels (reserve the marinade). Put the seasoned flour into a plastic bag and shake the hare pieces in it so that each piece is coated evenly. In a large frying pan, fry the bacon in the butter gently until the fat is rendered. Remove the bacon with a slotted spoon and reserve. Fry the pieces of hare briskly until they are browned all over, then place in a heavy Dutch oven. Sprinkle the bacon and crushed cloves over the hare.

Add any flour that is left to the juices in the pan; stir and cook gently until amalgamated with the fat. Add the marinade little by little and cook to simmering point, stirring and scraping the pan to mix in all the little bits. Add the tomato paste and the chocolate broken into little bits. Stir until all is mixed and melted. Season with salt and black pepper and pour over the hare.

Cover the Dutch oven tightly with foil and its lid. Place in a preheated oven at 300°F to cook for 3 hours. Half an hour before serving, add the sautéed mushrooms and onions and some forcemeat balls.

4 tablespoons butter

10 whole cloves, crushed

2 tablespoons tomato paste

3½ ounces unsweetened
chocolate

salt and freshly ground pepper

½ pound button mushrooms,
sautéed in butter

½ pound pearl onions or
shallots, sautéed in butter

FOR THE FORCEMEAT BALLS:

1⅓ cups dry white bread crumbs

¼ cup grated beef suet or butter

1 teaspoon grated lemon zest

1 teaspoon each minced fresh
parsley, thyme, and oregano

1 slice of cooked ham,
minced

1 egg, beaten

milk

hot pepper sauce or cayenne

olive oil

To make the forcemeat balls, which are well worth the effort, mix the bread crumbs with the suet or butter. Add the lemon zest, herbs, and ham. Add the egg and enough milk to bind the ingredients together but keeping the mixture firm. Season with a dash of hot pepper sauce or cayenne. Flour your hands and form walnut-sized balls. Fry in olive oil for 5 minutes to brown all over.

Serve the completed dish with a good red-currant jelly, a purée of celery root and potato (twice as much celery root as potatoes), and some fine little Brussels sprouts.

JP

HAUNCH OF VENISON IN CIDER

This recipe is from the Forest of Dean, where local venison is often cooked
in the local alcoholic cider.

a 2- to 3-pound haunch (leg
roast) of venison

2½ cups hard apple cider

flour

salt and freshly ground pepper

4 tablespoons butter

½ teaspoon ground allspice

bouquet garni

3 onions, chopped

2 carrots, chopped

⅓ cup venison stock

Marinate the venison in the cider overnight. Drain, retaining the
cider, and pat dry with paper towels. Flour the roast, season with
salt and pepper, and brown on all sides in the hot butter.

Place the venison in a Dutch oven and add all the remaining
ingredients, including the marinade. Cover and cook in a
preheated oven at 350°F for 2 hours.

Serve garnished with watercress.

CDW

MEDALLIONS OF VENISON WITH BLACKBERRY JELLY OR BLACKBERRIES

Try to get some well-aged venison if you like the gamey taste.

2–3 medallions of venison per person

sliced bacon, preferably unsmoked, cut into strips

flour seasoned with salt and pepper

the best blackberry jelly you can find or blackberries, red wine, and sugar

really good meat stock

sour cream or crème fraîche

salt and freshly ground pepper

Fry enough bacon very gently to render enough fat to fry the medallions. Remove the bacon pieces (you can sprinkle them on a salad). Put enough well-seasoned flour into a plastic bag and toss the pieces of venison in it; remove and lay on some wax paper. Heat the bacon drippings and fry the meat on a medium heat for 5–7 minutes, turning frequently. Put them in a warmed dish with a teaspoon of blackberry jelly on each medallion, and keep warm while you make the sauce.

If you are using blackberries instead of jelly, cook them lightly in a little red wine with sugar to taste. Spoon over the medallions as for the jelly.

Depending on how much you are cooking, add enough of the meat stock to the pan you fried the meat in. Boil briskly, stirring all the juices together. When it starts to look syrupy, mix in enough sour cream or crème fraîche to make a rich sauce. Adjust the seasoning. Pour over the venison.

Serve with tiny Brussels sprouts and egg noodles with chestnuts, if you have some handy. Applesauce can also be added as a side dish.

JP

Illustrated overleaf

PHEASANT AND PICKLED WALNUT TERRINE

The great advantage of this terrine is that it needs no forcemeat and is made entirely with pheasant, which in country areas, in particular, makes it very cheap.

1 pheasant

½ bottle of red vermouth

1 pound sliced bacon

salt and freshly ground pepper

1 jar of pickled walnuts

Remove the meat from the pheasant, chop into small pieces, and marinate in the red vermouth overnight.

Line a terrine mold with bacon slices. Drain the pheasant meat and arrange half in the mold. Season with salt and pepper. Put a layer of pickled walnuts on top and fill with the rest of the pheasant. Season. Cover with more bacon.

Set the mold in a water bath and cook in a preheated oven at 350°F for 45 minutes. When cooked, ease the terrine away from sides of the mold and leave to cool in the mold. Turn out for serving.

CDW

Clarissa's tip

Game must be hung, otherwise it has no flavor. The main thing is to keep the flies off it. It should be hung in a game cupboard or in a cheesecloth sack in a cool, dry place. If you want to know whether a pheasant has been adequately hung, pull a tail feather to see if it comes out.

TERRINE OF YOUNG GROUSE

Grouse is always expensive, even when the season has settled down. I absolutely love it, together with woodcock and snipe. I find these dark-meated gamebirds the most desirable. This is a way to make a brace of grouse into a truly great first course, sufficient for 6–8 people.

2 young grouse

softened butter

salt and freshly ground black pepper

pork fatback or sliced bacon (preferably unsmoked) for wrapping

2 carrots, chopped

1 large onion, chopped

2 celery stalks, chopped

2 bayleaves

½ cup medium sherry

Worcestershire or Harvey's sauce

1 envelope unflavored gelatin

½ pound slab bacon, diced (about 1½ cups)

½ pound horse or cremini mushrooms, diced

fresh thyme

2 teaspoons red-currant jelly

Butter and season the grouse, wrap in the slices of fatback or bacon, and sit in a small, snug roasting pan with a cup of water. Cover loosely with foil so that the birds will be as much poached (in the cooking sense) as roasted and no cooking juices are wasted. Cook in a preheated oven at 425°F for 15–20 minutes. Remove from the oven and let them cool in their juices, then remove the meat from the bones and carve into nice slivers.

To make stock, put the bones and the juices from the pan in a saucepan with 2½ cups of water, the carrots, onion, celery, and bayleaves. Bring to a boil, then simmer very gently for about 2 hours with a lid on. Season to taste, and filter through a fine strainer. Return to the rinsed-out saucepan, add the sherry and a dash of Worcestershire sauce, and reduce to 2 cups of liquid. Take off the heat and dissolve the gelatin in the liquid, stirring like mad.

Sauté the diced bacon in a bit of butter, then toss in the mushrooms and stir-fry briefly. Add some chopped fresh thyme, if desired. Arrange alternate layers of grouse with the mushroom and bacon mixture in a terrine mold (or loaf pan). Pour the stock over just to cover the ingredients. Leave to set in the refrigerator.

Melt the red-currant jelly and spoon over the top as a glaze. Allow to set again. After you have unmolded the terrine, sprinkle with a little finely chopped parsley and a few random red currants, if you have them. Serve sliced, with warm brown toast and butter.

JP

Rabbit in Aspic

I am very fond of jellied food for summer festivities, *Jambon Persillé de Bourgogne* being one of the classic ones. This receipt using rabbit is a variation on the theme. The essential ingredient is a first class, homemade jellied stock.

really good jellied chicken or meat stock

1 wild or farmed rabbit, cut up

baby carrots, scrubbed and sliced

¼ cup dry vermouth

⅓ cup capers, chopped

parsley, chives, and tarragon

hard-cooked hen or quail eggs

anchovy fillets

It is essential to have a good jellied stock for this dish. I collect bones in the freezer until I have sufficient to make a good quantity of stock. Boil them with an onion, 2 carrots, 1 celery stalk, 2 bayleaves, and some crushed parsley stems for an hour; season with salt, strain, cool, and chill, then remove the solidified fat. If you want a really stiff jelly, add a chopped pig's foot.

Bring enough stock to cover the rabbit pieces to a boil. Drop the rabbit into the stock with the carrots and the vermouth. Turn the heat down and poach the contents gently until tender, 30–45 minutes (wild rabbit takes longer than tame). Check for seasoning. Remove the rabbit and carrots with a slotted spoon. When cool enough to handle, take the meat off the bone. Chill the stock enough to remove any fat from the top.

Cut the meat into goodly chunks, mix into the stock, and add the carrots. Mix in the capers and a generous amount of herbs, all minced. Pour the lot into a charming mold (maybe one of those rabbit ones) and chill until set. If you are doubtful as to the stiffness of your stock you could add some unflavored gelatin when the stock is still hot after the poaching.

Unmold onto a suitable dish and surround with the quail eggs or quartered hen eggs. Decorate with anchovy fillets and serve with a potato salad dressed with olive oil, Dijon mustard, and lemon juice.

JP

Clarissa's strangest kill

JENNIFER: I ate peacock once. It's rather like pheasant.

CLARISSA: It is a bit. I once shot one in my sprouting broccoli. It was an accident, of course. Rabbits were always getting into my garden, so I used to throw up the kitchen window and shoot them from there. But one day, what I thought was a rabbit turned out to be a peacock.

JENNIFER: Whose peacock was it?

CLARISSA: It belonged to the people next door.

JENNIFER: They must have been pleased!

CLARISSA: Well, I asked them to dinner and we had rather a good bottle of wine. Then they said, this is very interesting, what is it? Well, I said, I didn't buy it at Harrod's.

Lock up your peacocks when Clarissa's around

$\mathscr{F}$OOD IN THE WILD

CLARISSA WRITES: I have a favorite cartoon, which shows a picture of a mother battling against the storm, her hair streaming out behind her, clutching the hand of her small son who is clearly in danger of being blown away. The caption below reads: "Despite every adversity the British shall barbecue!" As the shots of Jennifer and me cooking mussels on the beach show, we are no exception to this adage. Jennifer has a much more glamorous past in this area – picnics on the Yangtze River, diving for sea urchins in Taormina, *al fresco* picnics with footmen and gold plate in Portugal – but even so we both love it.

Two in a tent:
Clarissa tries to persuade
Jennifer of the joys of camping

My friend Claire Macdonald has an annual Boxing Day picnic on the beach in Scotland, with everyone wrapped up warm and a huge bonfire built out of the wind. It makes such a change from the lavishness of Christmas Day.

My first picnic memory is of sitting in the woods of the Royal Horticultural Society gardens at Wisley. I must have been four years old, eating cold sausages, which tasted wonderful. But outdoor food is not just picnics – it is barbecues and luaus, formal *al fresco* meals, and searching for wild food in the woods. One of the best things I ever ate was a young, uncurled, still white bracken frond in tempura batter. I admit that I ate it at Alastair Little's restaurant, but it is quite feasible to make it out of doors.

When I worked on a pheasant farm, the woods were full of mushrooms, which I used to go out and pick. The entire village waited for me to die in agony. When I didn't they eventually allowed me to feed them some of my harvest. Today mushroom picking is much more widely spread, but it is especially lovely in

Scotland. I pick inkcaps fresh from my drive in the morning, and when I visit friends they beg me to take a bag home as they have too many!

This program is still in the mind and fantasy of the director. All I know is it involves Scouts (see my story of the silver penknife), possibly the Isle of Mull, and possibly a luau. My dreams are filled by Scouts in grass skirts playing bagpipes and heating rocks, but we shall see.

In middle age I have discovered camping. My greatest friend from school (she of the baking weekend) dragged me off with my godson to a wet weekend on Lake Bala, and I fell in love with "roughing it." Mine was a deprived childhood, of the Ritz in Madrid and the Lido in Venice. Now I have bought a tent and have never looked back – I am a dab hand at cooking steak with foie gras over butane gas. One mustn't lose sight of one's principles. It is, however, a proper ridge tent (a three-man one – you never know), with two bell ends to cook under if the weather gets rough.

The other thing I am a dab hand at is grilling whole sheep, which is very useful if you have a lot of friends. The interesting thing is it still takes 20 minutes per pound!

The story of the silver penknife

There was once a great beauty who was courted by every man in the land. A very rich admirer wanted to buy her a present and asked what she would like. He offered her diamonds, pearls, rubies, and emeralds, but all she wanted was a silver penknife. He tried to insist on something more precious, but all she wanted was the penknife. So he bought her a silver penknife.

She was delighted, but when she went to put it away in a drawer, he noticed that it was full of silver penknives. "Why," he asks, "when you already have so many penknives, do you want another one?" She replied, "My darling, I may be young and beautiful now, with men falling at my feet, but when I am old and ugly, I know what a Boy Scout will do for a silver penknife."

*W*ILD MUSHROOM PANCAKES

When you have risen from your tent and gathered your mushrooms, this is an easy breakfast dish. You can even make the batter the night before. If there are no mushrooms, just have pancakes.

FOR THE BATTER:

1¼ cups self-rising flour

2 eggs

⅞ cup milk

salt and freshly ground pepper

¾ pound fresh wild mushrooms

4 tablespoons butter

oil

Make the batter, adding seasoning to taste, and leave to stand for at least 1 hour.

Melt the butter in a frying pan and cook the mushrooms until they are wilted and all liquid has evaporated. Set aside to cool.

Mix together the batter and mushrooms. Heat a frying pan, put in a smidgen of oil, and fry pancakes about 2 inches in diameter. Eat.

CDW

SCALLOP AND BACON KEBAB

I first tasted this cooked out of doors by Johnnie Noble at his Loch Fyne Seafood Festival. Whether it was the undoubted quality of his scallops, the taste of the Ayrshire bacon, or the scenic beauty, it seemed to me I could happily spend eternity eating this dish. To hell with ambrosia!

Any simple dish is only as good as the quality of its ingredients. You may be restrained by your locality as to the scallops, but there is nowhere where you cannot buy fine bacon if you look for it. Buy lean, center-cut bacon that is thick sliced, or use *pancetta*, the Italian bacon.

PER SKEWER:

2 sea scallops, cut in half

bacon slices

4 slices of strong onion

Wrap each scallop in bacon and slide onto the skewer, inserting a piece of onion between each scallop.

Cook over a charcoal fire or under the broiler until the bacon is cooked, turning from time to time. Devour.

CDW

FRITTATA WITH TOMATOES, ONIONS AND BASIL

If you have a charcoal fire going, you can make this "omelet" outside; otherwise make it at home and take it with you – it is particularly good cold. I ate it first in Tuscany, where it can have many variations – it is an excellent way of using up any leftover vegetables, pasta, ham, and cheese. Very different to the rapid cooking of a French omelet, this flat Italian version is cooked over a low heat, very gently, so is very easy to cook when doing other tasks.

6 medium onions, thinly sliced

6 tablespoons olive oil

½ pound plum tomatoes

salt and freshly ground pepper

6 extra large eggs

2 tablespoons freshly grated Parmesan cheese

a handful of fresh basil

4 tablespoons butter

Sweat the onions in the oil until quite soft and just browning. Skin and chop the tomatoes (you can also use 1 cup drained canned ones) and add to the onions with a little salt to taste. Cook for 10 minutes, stirring occasionally. Press the vegetables to the side of the pan and remove to a bowl using a slotted spoon. Leave to cool.

Beat the eggs until well mixed but not frothy. Add the vegetables, cheese, a good quantity of ground black pepper, and more salt to your liking. Tear up the basil leaves, add, and stir everything together. Melt the butter in a 12-inch nonstick frying pan until it is just foaming. Pour in the egg mixture, lower the heat, and cook for about 15 minutes until the eggs are set but the top is still a bit runny. Then you can put the pan under the broiler for half a minute.

Loosen the frittata with a metal spatula and slide onto a suitable dish. Cut into wedges when cooled. It can be eaten warm with a salad or cold on a hunk of bread, as the schoolchildren and the workmen do for their lunch.

JP

Illustrated overleaf

SHOOTER'S SANDWICH

This wonderful sandwich has stood me in good stead on many journeys. Indeed, it fed one of my editors and his wife all the way to Rome. It comes from a charming book by T. Earle Welby, *The Dinner Knell* (Methuen, 1932). It is a great standby on British trains, where the buffet is temperamental to say the least. I always carry my own food and drink, together with ice and napkins.

a very thick boneless sirloin steak the size of the loaf

1 unsliced loaf of the best quality

some portobello mushrooms

salt and freshly ground black pepper

The steak should be 1½–2 inches thick, cut from some fine well-hung animal. Cut one end off the loaf and remove as much center crumb as necessary to allow the steak and mushrooms to fit in snugly when cooked. Grill (or broil) the meat fiercely on either side, but keep it very rare. Take from the fire and season well on both sides, then insert it into the hollowed loaf. Grill (or broil) enough mushrooms to cover the meat plentifully and place them over the steak. Replace the deleted crust end of the loaf.

Wrap the whole thing in a double sheet of white blotting paper and secure with string into a neat parcel. Then secure again with wax paper and more string. (Nowadays you could use foil and film, but it is not so charmful.) Place under a weighted board for at least 6 hours. When eating this sandwich, just cut off a slice as required. As Welby said, "With this 'Sandwich' and a flask of whiskey waters, a man may travel from Land's End to Quaker Oats (sic) and snap his fingers at both."

JP

STRAWBERRY AND CHOCOLATE FONDUE

Fondues were always a feature of my childhood, as we went skiing every year. I loved the suspense of not dropping my dipper. As I got older, I loved the bottle of wine when someone else dropped theirs, and the alternative of the kiss from some snow-bronzed hunk. Today I just like fondues.

12 ounces bittersweet or semisweet chocolate

1 cup heavy cream

2 tablespoons brandy or rum

a bowl of strawberries, unhulled

In your fondue pot, melt the chocolate and cream together, then slowly stir in the alcohol. If, like me, you are allergic to alcohol, either use orange juice with a dash of balsamic vinegar or boil the alcohol separately before adding it to the fondue.

Holding your strawberry by the stalk, dip it into the mixture and twirl it about. Remember the penalty if you drop it. Pause a moment to allow the chocolate to cool slightly, and then devour.

CDW

CHEESE FONDUE

Use the cheeses suggested or any other mixture of hard and soft cheeses
you might fancy.

7 ounces each of Gruyère, Emmentaler, and Vacherin cheese

1 garlic clove, sliced

1¼ cups dry white wine

juice of 1 lemon

freshly grated nutmeg

2 teaspoons cornstarch

a small glass of kirsch

freshly ground black pepper

good bread, cut into cubes

Grate the Gruyère and the Emmentaler, but cut the Vacherin into small pieces. Place all the cheese into an enameled or flameproof earthenware pot. Add the garlic, wine, lemon juice, and a good scraping of nutmeg. Mix the cornstarch to a smooth paste with the kirsch and stir into the pot. Bring the mixture slowly to a boil, stirring all the time. Turn down the heat and simmer softly for 4 minutes. Season well with freshly ground pepper and transfer to a candle or spirit burner on the table.

The fondue should be stirred by the eaters while the dish is being consumed, with forks or spears holding the cubes of bread. This will avoid curdling and bottom burning. When you are nearing the end you will find a delicious crust on the bottom of the pot, which is a great treat. You will only need a salad and some fruit after this rich affair.

JP

CÈPE & COCKLE SOUP

This is a great soup, and the changes can be rung with any shellfish and any wild mushrooms. In the wild you just make it as a soup, but once you have an oven the dinner party version has a puff-pastry cover.

4 scallions, minced

1 celery stalk, minced

4 sprigs of fresh thyme

2 tablespoons unsalted butter

4 ounces fresh cèpes
(Boletus edulis),
roughly chopped

6 ounces oyster mushrooms,
roughly chopped

salt and freshly ground pepper

2 cups milk

1½ cups shucked cockles or
small hardshell clams

¾ cup diced cooked potato

FOR THE POSH INDOOR VERSION:

1 egg, beaten

¾ pound puff pastry, thawed

3 tablespoons celery or sesame
seeds

In a saucepan, sauté the scallions, celery, and thyme in the butter for 2–3 minutes. Add the mushrooms and soften till the juices run. Season with salt and pepper. Pour the milk over, bring to a simmer, and add the cockles and diced potato. Heat through and serve.

If you are making the posh dinner party version, make the soup as above and then ladle into four ovenproof soup bowls. Moisten the rims of the bowls with beaten egg and give each a puff-pastry lid. Brush with more egg and sprinkle on celery or sesame seeds. Bake in a preheated oven at 425°F for 35–40 minutes until the lid is risen and golden brown. Serve at once.

CDW

ℛOQUEBRUNE TARTINE

This picnic loaf is a meal in itself, extremely healthy and full of flavor.

1 long French baguette

garlic cloves

salt and freshly ground pepper

10 black olives, pitted

1 red bell pepper, minced

2 tomatoes

a handful of green beans, cooked

4 anchovy fillets

2 tablespoons olive oil

lemon juice

Cut the bread in half, lengthwise. Smash as much garlic as you fancy with a little salt and rub it into the cut surfaces. Mash together the olives, red pepper, tomatoes, green beans, and anchovies. Add the olive oil and lemon juice to taste. Adjust seasoning, grinding a lot of black pepper into the mixture. Blend everything together, then spread on the baguette. Sandwich the sides together, wrap thoroughly in foil, and put under a weighted pastry board for at least an hour so that the flavors can soak into the bread. At the picnic, cut the loaf into good chunks and hand around.

JP

MUTTACHAR (SPICED EGGS)

My step-grandfather was a Sephardic Jew from Calcutta, with the splendid Biblical name of Ezechial Manasseh. When he went to handle the family's jute interests in the Far East, his mother sent him a cook called Fuzdah, who was a "black Jew" from Cochin. This recipe, for which I searched long and hard, is one of Fuzdah's Cochin dishes. The unusual aspect is that where most recipes use hard-cooked eggs, this dish allows as an alternative that the eggs be poached in the liquid.

1 tablespoon oil

1 small onion, chopped

1 hot green chili pepper, seeded and chopped

1 ripe tomato, sliced

½ green mango, sliced (optional)

2½ cups coconut milk and water, mixed in equal parts

¼ teaspoon each turmeric, paprika, and ground cilantro

salt

10 fresh curry leaves

a handful of chopped fresh cilantro

juice of ½ lemon

4 eggs, hard cooked or raw

In a heavy frying pan, heat the oil and sauté the onion till golden. Add the chili, tomato, and mango and fry a little longer. Pour in the coconut milk and water and bring to a boil. Add the turmeric, paprika, ground cilantro, and salt to taste, and simmer for 5–10 minutes.

Rub the curry leaves between your palms to release the flavor, and add them and the fresh cilantro to the mixture. Add the lemon juice and simmer for a further 10 minutes.

If you are using the eggs hard-cooked, add them to the sauce and heat through for about 5 minutes. If to be poached, break the eggs gently into the mixture and cook for about 3 minutes.

This dish can be served with rice or with snippets of toast or good bread to mop up the delicious juice.

CDW

GRILLED MACKEREL WITH DIJON MUSTARD

If you chance upon a fishing village or a pier where really fresh mackerel can be caught, catch or beguile enough of the fine creatures as will feed your company. Clean the guts out and make three deep incisions on either side of the backbone. Salt these wounds well, as well as the interior of the fish. Spread liberally with Dijon mustard and crushed fennel seed if you have some about your person, or gather it wild from the hedgerows. Make a fire and broil the fish on some chicken wire or any other device you can find. With a good heat going, they should take about 4–5 minutes on each side.

JP

POTTED CRAB OR LOBSTER

Potting is an old way of preserving meat or fish. We all eat *rillettes* or *confit de canard* with glee, but forget our own British heritage. Almost anything can be potted, and, in Scotland, the butcher's shops sell potted hough, which is potted beef shank. I particularly like potted crab, which I think makes an excellent appetizer or light lunch dish. Potted lobster I once served as the savory course at the end of a rather elaborate dinner party I did for the *London Evening Standard*. It was very well received!

**3 large cooked crabs or
2 cooked lobsters**

**½ cup clarified butter
(see page 30)**

½ teaspoon ground mace

juice of 1 lemon

salt and freshly ground pepper

Remove the meat from the shellfish. Keep any coral separate.

For potted crab: Melt half the butter in a frying pan, add the crab meat, and mash with a fork. Add the mace and lemon juice, and season with salt and pepper. Taste and adjust the seasoning. Put into ramekin dishes, cover with the rest of the clarified butter, and leave to set. Alternatively, melt all the butter, proceed as before, and return the crab mixture to its shell. I prefer this as a main course for a light meal.

For potted lobster: Proceed as for crab, but layer the coral and the meat in the ramekin dishes.

CDW

*S*PAGHETTI ESTIVI FREDDI (SUMMER SPAGHETTI – COLD)

Originally from the Isle of Ischia, this is a Roman spaghetti salad.

3 plump garlic cloves, minced

5 tablespoons best olive oil

a handful of fresh mint leaves (spearmint is best), minced

5 tablespoons fresh orange juice

12 black olives

6 anchovy fillets

1 small jar marinated mushrooms in oil

salt

1½ pounds spaghetti

Cook the garlic gently in the oil until golden. Add the mint and take off the heat. Pour in the orange juice. Chop the olives and anchovies roughly and stir into the pan, then add the mushrooms. Season with salt and mix all together.

Cook the spaghetti in lots of boiling water, keeping them slightly more *al dente* than usual. Drain and pour onto a large platter. Mix in the sauce and spread out to cool. When cool, transfer to a nice rustic bowl to serve outside.

JP

Illustrated overleaf

Bratwurst and Blue Cheese Salad with Mustard Dressing

This dish came about when I was trying to design an interesting menu for the launch of a German supermarket chain. They kept sending me food I didn't want, including a box of bratwurst. The recipe has to have been a result of divine intervention because nothing good would have been inspired by my thoughts as I looked at these sausages.

6 bratwurst

bacon drippings, or oil

½ pound strong blue cheese
(I used Fourme d'Ambert)

olive oil

white wine vinegar

2 tablespoons German mustard

sugar

salt and freshly ground pepper

Fry the bratwurst in a little bacon drippings (or oil will do) until lightly colored all over. Chop into 1-inch pieces, removing any loose skin. Roughly chop the cheese.

Make a dressing with the oil, vinegar, and mustard. You will need a strong, fairly dense dressing, so add a pinch of sugar, if desired. Season with salt and pepper.

Mix the dressing with the bratwurst and cheese, cover, and leave overnight before serving.

CDW

*S*TRAWBERRY SALAD

For a ravishingly pretty salad to go with a cold fowl or fish, peel a cucumber (or as many as you require) and slice very thinly on a mandolin, if you have one; or do it by eye with a sharp knife. Sprinkle with a little salt and place between two plates with a weight on top for an hour or so, pouring off the liquid at intervals. Cut an equal amount of strawberries into horizontal slices, grind some black pepper over them, and sprinkle with a little lemon juice or balsamic vinegar. Just before you eat, mix the two ingredients together.

JP

FRANKFURTER, PICKLED BEETS AND HORSERADISH SALAD

Jewish cooking has a wonderful thing called *khrame*, which is horseradish sauce with beets.
It is probably this that made me think of this combination.

6 frankfurters

6 small pickled beets, drained and chopped

2 onions, chopped

2 teaspoons capers

olive oil

wine vinegar

½ teaspoon finely grated fresh horseradish, or 1 teaspoon bottled red horseradish

salt and freshly ground pepper

Put your frankfurters into boiling water, bring back to a boil, remove from the heat, and leave for 10 minutes. Drain, chop, and place in a bowl with the beets, onions and capers.

Make a dressing with the remaining ingredients. Be sparing with the vinegar as the beets will be tart. If using fresh horseradish, the most painless way to grate it is in a food processor, but be careful when you remove the lid. Add a little cream to the horseradish before adding it to the dressing if you find it too strong.

Mix the dressing with the frankfurter mixture. Cover and leave overnight before serving.

CDW

Illustrated on previous pages

 POTATO SALAD

A really good potato salad, green with herbs and well dressed – not that disgusting mess that is covered in some terrible white glue – is always a welcome dish outdoors.

Whichever potatoes you buy, let them be firm and waxy. Simply boil them in their skins. Have ready a large bowl with a sufficient quantity of best olive oil to dress generously the amount of potatoes you have cooked, and season with salt, freshly ground pepper, and the tiniest bit of white wine vinegar. Peel the potatoes when cool enough to handle and place immediately in the dressing. Wait until they are cold if you wish to cut them smaller, or they tend to crumble.

Now the all-important part. Chop a vast bunch of parsley, tarragon, chives, and scallions fairly finely and mix into the potatoes. The scent from the resulting mixture is wonderful. Finely grated lemon zest sprinkled on top is another fragrant addition.

A UAU

The idea of building a pit to cook in is as old as time. What you cook in it can be as complicated or as easy as you want, and its size can be whatever the labor force allows – a much better usage for Scout bob-a-job week than ruining the paintwork on your car. Suggestions for food to cook in the pit are ears of corn, potatoes, fish fillets wrapped in foil with butter and seasoning, chops or sausages wrapped in foil, clams, mussels, or lobsters. Use your imagination, and experiment.

1. Drive four posts into the ground to delineate a rectangular area about 5 by 8 feet. Dig out to a depth of 18 inches, banking the sand or earth around the edges.

2. Line the pit with smooth, dry pebbles (bricks will also do).

3. Start a small fire on top of the stones in the middle and gradually add logs until you fill the whole pit.

4. Keep the fire stoked for at least an hour, then allow to burn down for another hour to ensure the stones are properly heated.

5. Carefully rake the embers from the pit without disturbing the stones.

6. As quickly as possible, spread well-rinsed seaweed or non-poisonous green leaves over the stones in a layer about 6 inches deep.

7. Lay the prepared food in a single layer on top of the seaweed or leaves.

8. Spread a 6-inch layer of seaweed or leaves over the food. Make sure the food is completely covered.

9. Cover with a tarpaulin that extends at least a foot beyond the sides of the pit. Weigh down the edges with stones. Let the food cook for at least 3 hours.

CDW

KORDALIA

Skordalia is a Greek version of *ailoli* mayonnaise, but made without eggs. It goes well with fish, fowl, or vegetables and is most useful as a picnic sauce instead of mayonnaise, which goes lethal if left in the sun, producing salmonella.

3 fat garlic cloves

a 2-inch thick slice of stale white bread, de-crusted

¾ cup blanched almonds, grated or finely chopped

½ cup olive oil

salt

wine vinegar

Crush the garlic well in a mortar. Soak the bread in water, then squeeze out the surplus. Add to the garlic in the mortar and pound away, gradually mixing in the grated almonds until you have a nice homogenous paste. Start adding the oil drop by drop as for mayonnaise and finishing with a steady stream. Finally, season with salt and vinegar to your taste.

JP

Cooking a Whole Beast on a Spit

Over the last 9 years, this is something I have been asked to advise on regularly, and in the last 4 months, since we opened our shop in Edinburgh, I have been asked twice and helped do it once. It is a good idea for a party. I once cooked two sheep and four sucking pigs for a party I gave in London. It is a surprisingly cheap way of catering and always causes excitement.

1. Either hire a spit and stand, or build two pillars of concrete blocks, each 3 feet high and 4 feet apart.

2. Make a marinade of garlic, herbs, lemon, and oil and rub it well into the animal. If it is a sheep, put branches of rosemary inside the body cavity and rub in coarse salt. If a pig, you can put garlic and herbs inside and sew up the cavity.

3. Push the spit or a ½-inch diameter steel rod through the animal's anus and out through its mouth, or throat if the head is removed.

4. Bind the pig's feet to the spit with steel wire (this does not apply to sheep).

5. Light a fire between the posts, using a mixture of wood and charcoal, and spread it out. The fire should be about 8 inches deep. Leave to burn for about 2 hours.

6. Raise the spit in place over the fire and secure to the stand or pillars. After 20 minutes of cooking, the fat will begin to run, so baste with the marinade. Continue to baste every half hour. Raising or lowering the spit above the coals will control the cooking.

A lamb weighs between 11 and 50 pounds, and a pig 8 to 150 pounds, although anything above 70 pounds is impractical. Allow a minimum of 3 hours' cooking for a small beast; otherwise calculate at 20 minutes to each pound.

CDW

It's not just the food that's
wild …

'Shall I be mother?" Jennifer
pours as Clarissa ponders on
where to dig her luau pit

INDEX

PICTURE ACKNOWLEDGMENTS

Jason Bell pp. 3, 42, 95, 126, 155,
156, 185 (bottom)

John Garrett p. 192

James Murphy © pp. 19, 27, 31,
34–35, 51, 55, 59, 66–67, 71, 75, 83,
86–87, 98–99, 103, 110–111, 119,
130–131, 135, 143, 150–151, 159,
162–163, 171–172, 174–175

Optomen Television pp. 8–9, 11, 12,
13, 14, 40, 41, 43, 68, 69, 81, 92–93,
125, 185 (top)